SENSATIONAL SACHETS

SEWING SCENTED TREASURES

by Stephanie Valley

SENSATIONAL SACHETS

SEWING SCENTED TREASURES

by Stephanie Valley

Sterling Publishing Co., Inc.
New York

A STERLING/SEWING INFORMATION RESOURCES BOOK

Sewing Information Resources

Owner: JoAnn Pugh-Gannon

Photography: Nathan Ham Photography

Book design and graphics: Rose Sheifer, Graphic Productions

Pattern illustrations: Janet White

Index: Anne Leach

Sewing Information Resources is a registered trademark of GANZ Inc.
Library of Congress Cataloging-in-Publication Data
Valley, Stephanie.
          Sensational sachets : sewing scented treasures / by Stephanie Valley.
              p. cn. — (Great sewing projects series)
          "A Sterling/Sewing Information Resources book".
          Includes index.
          ISBN 0-8069-9810-5
          1. Machine sewing. 2. Potpourris (Scented floral mixtures)
          3. Notions (Merchandise) I. Title. II. Series.
TT715.V35   1997   96-39315
746.9—DC21   CIP

A Sterling/Sewing Information Resources Book

2 4 6 8 10 9 7 5 3 1

Published by Sterling Publishing Company, Inc.
387 Park Avenue South, New York, N.Y. 10016
Produced by Sewing Information Resources
P.O. Box 330, Wasco, Il. 60183
©1997 by Stephanie Valley
Distributed in Canada by Sterling Publishing
c/o Canadian Manda Group, One Atlantic Avenue, Suite 105
Toronto, Ontario, Canada, N6K 3E7
Distributed in Great Britain and Europe by Cassell PLC
Wellington House, 125 Strand, London WC2R 0BB, England
Distributed in Australia by Capricorn Link (Australia) Pty Ltd.
P.O. Box 6651, Baulkham Hills, Business Centre, NSW 2153, Australia

Printed in Hong Kong
All rights reserved
Sterling ISBN 0-8069-9810-5

DEDICATION

I would like to dedicate this book to my parents,

Paul and Jeanne Hoferer. Thank you for encouraging my

creative spirit even when it didn't seem like the sensible

thing to do, and for your never-ending love and support.

I would also like to thank Linda Lee who has opened

doors for me that I never knew existed.

TABLE OF CONTENTS

Chapter IV

Chapter V

INTRODUCTION

If someone would have told me five years ago that I would be writing a book on sewing sachets, I would have thought they were crazy. Five years ago, I was taking my first sewing class and was just beginning to understand what a seam allowance was and the meaning of grainline.

I didn't start learning to sew until my senior year in college. I majored in textile design at the University of Kansas. I had a lot of fabrics that I had created just piled up in my closets. These pieces of cloth represented hours of my time and labor and I wanted to make something with them. Learning to sew seamed like the only way to make that possible.

My mother had never sewn but since my grandmother had for years, it was to her that I turned for help. She got me started and also furnished me with my first sewing machine, purchased at a church sale for $50. It was a fancy machine, unlike hers, it would zigzag and backstitch!

That machine got me through my first, beginning sewing class at a local fabric store, but since then I have purchased a sewing machine—with all the necessary "bells and whistles." I also ended up getting a job at the same fabric store where I was taking classes and so began my introduction into the world of fabric collecting. I must confess I am an addict, not only to fabric, but to beads, buttons, ribbons and trims.

Along with a new closet full of "stuff," sewing opened up many creative avenues to which I had not previously been exposed. I had seen a few sachets in catalogs and magazines before I became fully intrigued and determined to make one myself. Here was a project that was small, didn't have to fit anyone, and could incorporate all of the fabrics and embellishments I had collected in my closets. And to top that off, they smelled good and made wonderful gifts.

I created that first sachet about three years ago and my sewing room has smelled like potpourri ever since. The more sachets I make the more ideas I have for new ones. There is something about these small scented packages, that you make with your own hand, out of materials you love, that is intimate and good for the creative soul!

CHAPTER 1

INGREDIENTS AND SOURCES

ACHETS ARE SCENTED PACKAGES, SMALL ENOUGH TO FIT IN YOUR HAND OR DRESSER DRAWER. MAYBE IT'S THE SIZE THAT MAKES SACHETS SO WONDERFUL, OR MAYBE IT'S THE SCENT. WHATEVER THE REASON, SACHETS HAVE BEEN AROUND SINCE THE SIXTEENTH CENTURY WHEN THEY WERE FITTED INTO CLOTHES AND BEDDING AS INSECT REPELLENTS. VICTORIAN WOMEN WERE ESPECIALLY FOND OF SACHETS. THEY TIED THEM IN THEIR SKIRTS, HUNG THEM ON FURNITURE AND TUCKED THEM BETWEEN THEIR LINENS. NO ROOM WAS LEFT UNSCENTED.

TODAY, THERE IS A RENEWED INTEREST BOTH IN NATURE AND HAND-CRAFTED ITEMS. PEOPLE ARE ONCE AGAIN INTERESTED IN MAKING THINGS THEMSELVES AND PRODUCING SOMETHING OF QUALITY FOR GIFTS OR FAMILY HEIRLOOMS. THERE IS NO BETTER PERSONAL SATISFACTION THAN CREATING SOMETHING OUT OF NOTHING. MAKING SACHETS DOES NOT REQUIRE ADVANCED SEWING SKILLS OR EVEN A GARDEN. THE INGREDIENTS AND SOURCES FOR THE PACKAGE AND THE SCENT ARE VERY SIMPLE.

The package and the scent of the sachet are equally important and the two should compliment one another. When selecting materials, consider the person the sachet is intended for or its destination. A man may not appreciate a frilly package or a flowery scent, and a sachet intended for a linen closet should not lose its charm when linens are stacked on top of it.

Natural fibers such as cotton, linen and silk are preferable fabrics for making sachets. These fabrics let the scent breathe and are more in harmony with the natural ingredients of the potpourri inside.

Silk is a wonderful fabric for sachets because of its luscious colorations and textures. There is great variety of silks available today at fine fabric stores and through many mail-order sources. Some of the mail-order sources will send you swatches for a small fee. Contrary to what is often recommended, most silks can be washed and their character is sometimes enhanced by this process. Silk prints with intense colors are the exception and should be tested first for color bleeding. The following silks are especially suited for sachets:

Douppioni: A firm, plain-weave fabric with irregular yarn slubs, becomes soft and drapey when washed.

Charmeuse: A soft, satin-weave fabric with a dull back and lustrous face.

Satin: A firmly woven, satin-weave fabric with a very smooth face.

Organza: A transparent, lightweight, firmly woven plain-weave fabric.

Special care should be taken when stitching and working with silk. It is a strong fiber but can cause stitching problems because of its texture.

Needles: Use size 60/8 for fine silks such as charmeuse and organza, size 70/10 for medium weight silks like doupioni.

Pins: Select fine glass head silk pins.

Thread: Cotton thread is recommended for all natural fibers, such as silk, linen, cotton and wool. Cotton embroidery thread should be used with fine silks.

Sewing machine stitch length: Use a small stitch length of 1.75 - 2mm.

Purchase small pieces or remnants of expensive fabrics that you would not normally buy in larger quantities. Remember, a quarter of a yard can go a long way in making a sachet. Save scraps from other projects and develop a stash of fabrics that will inspire you.

In addition to fabric, start collecting embellishments for your packages. Embellishments can be old or new, small or large, and sometimes on their own they might seem plain. Most fabric and craft stores will have at least a small selection of trims, ribbons, beads and buttons. For more unusual embellishments, check local flea markets for vintage finds or try fabric and notion mail-order sources.

Ribbons make wonderful embellishments and are available in a wide variety of colors, textures and widths. Ombré or variegated ribbons are perfect for making flowers and cocards. Grosgrain and velvet ribbons provide a more tailored appearance to a sachet because of their crispness. Wide, decorative embroidered ribbons can be made into a simple tube sachet. Paper florist ribbons are not desirable because of their brittle nature. Select whatever you are drawn to and what compliments the package fabric.

Adding small details like beads is a simple and inexpensive way to make a sachet look ornate. Bugle and seed beads come in a wide range of colors and sizes. Use them to embellish simple trim or ribbons. Large glass beads, used sparingly, add the perfect finishing touch to corners and ends of sachets. When combined, small amounts of trim, ribbons, beads and buttons can transform plain fabric into unique, ornamental packages.

THE SCENT

Sachets appeal to both our sense of sight and smell. We react to scents in our environment every day. They can recreate a time, a place or an event tucked in our memory. Nothing smells quite like freshly cut grass on a warm summer morning or the smoke of a roaring fire in the middle of winter. Our emotions and memories are intertwined with our sense of smell.

Potpourri, a mixture of dried flowers, leaves, herbs and spices, is one way of capturing our scent memories. Prepackaged potpourris are available in fine department and bath stores. Many of them have a nice presentation but their smell can be overly perfumed and does not last long. An especially popular prepackaged potpourri is Bitter Orange from Agraria in San Francisco. The scent is wonderfully fresh and lasts for years, which is the test of fine ingredients. The elements are a little large for some

sachets, but the orange and cinnamon pieces can be removed or broken down.

If you are adventurous and wish to make your own potpourri there are many resources available for recipes and instructions in the library and bookstores. You do not need a garden to make your own potpourri. There are several mail-order sources for all the necessary ingredients such as the San Francisco Herb Co., which even includes potpourri recipes in its catalog.

To make your own potpourri, you will need ingredients from the four major elements: flowers and leaves, herbs and spices, fixatives, and essential oils.

Flowers and leaves can be gathered in the garden, purchased at a florist shop or ordered through the mail. Once collected, they must be completely dried to corn flake crispness. Any dampness in the potpourri can cause the mixture to mildew.

Herbs and spices such as rosemary, coriander, cinnamon and cloves can be gathered from the garden, found in supermarkets or mail-ordered. These too must be bone-dry to prevent the potpourri from spoiling.

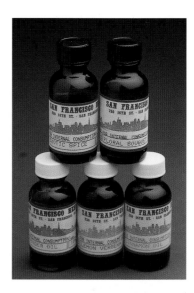

Fixatives are the elements used to absorb and retain the essential oils. Without a fixative the potpourri would lose its scent quickly. Orrisroot, oak moss, and benzoin are popular fixatives available through many mail-order sources.

Essential oils are the pure perfumed oils extracted from flowers, spices or herbs. A single oil can be used in a potpourri or you might try a combination of complimentary scents. Use natural, not synthetic oil whenever possible. Oils can be found in fine bath stores and mail-order catalogs.

There are endless ways that these four elements can be combined. Personal preference becomes the deciding factor since scent effects everyone differently. For most sachet bags, select recipes that call for small elements, not large cinnamon sticks or pine cones because they don't easily fit into the bags.

Here are two easy recipes to start with, developed by Topeka horticulturist Barbara Shapiro.

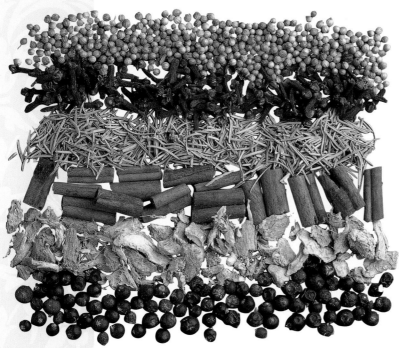

Lavender and Spice

3 cups - lavender

1 cup - blue corn flowers

1 cup - cloves

1 cup - cinnamon chips

1 cup - white or purple globe amaranths

1 cup - orrisroot

1 ounce - lavender oil

Summer Garden

4 cups - roses

1 cup - lavender

1 cup - yellow statice

2 cups - purple globe amaranths

1 cup - uva ursi leaves

1 cup - cinnamon

1 cup - orrisroot

1 ounce - rose oil

In a plastic or glass bowl that is not used for food, add the essential oil to the fixative (e.g., orrisroot in the above recipes) using an eye-dropper. Mix the remaining ingredients together in a large plastic or paper bag. Add the fixative with oil to the ingredients in the bag and stir gently to avoid crushing the flowers or leaves. Seal the bag and place it in a dry, dark, cool place to cure for a minimum of two weeks. Stir the mixture every two days to mingle the scents with each other. After the potpourri has cured it is ready to be used in your favorite sachet.

There are some shortcuts that can be taken to add scent to a sachet. Orrisroot or buckwheat can be scented with a few drops of essential oil and used on their own as a perfumed filler. Orrisroot works well in small bags when regular potpourri would be too large. Victorian ladies used scented buckwheat to fill their sachet bags. It

has a nice beanbag feel and weight and is available in health food stores. A popular alternative to potpourri for a man's or holiday sachet is balsam needles. The needles have a wonderful winter scent that will last for a year.

Getting the potpourri into the sachet can be the most challenging part of the project. Canning funnels will accomplish the task in most cases and may be purchased at the supermarket. However, sometimes the neck of the sachet bag is just a little too small. If that is the case, a funnel with a wider neck can be made by rolling up a sheet of paper and securing it with tape. No matter what your tool is or how careful you are, some of the potpourri will spill. Fill your sachet over a cookie sheet with a lip so the potpourri can be saved and reused.

In the following chapters you will find instructions for making a variety of sachets from the very simplistic "Sweet Roll" to the more elaborate "Leaves and Buds." Suggestions are given for materials and filler but remember there is no wrong combination. Most importantly, have fun, relax and enjoy the creative experience of making beautiful sachets.

CHAPTER 2

MACHINE TECHNIQUES

DD A PERSONAL TOUCH TO A SACHET PACKAGE BY INCORPORATING A SEWING MACHINE TECHNIQUE, SUCH AS PINTUCKING, COUCHING, BOBBIN-WORK OR HEMSTITCHING. THESE TECHNIQUES CAN BE TIME-CONSUMING WHEN APPLIED TO LARGER PROJECTS BUT ON A SMALLER ITEM, LIKE SACHETS, YOU CAN EXPERIMENT WITH-OUT SACRIFICING YOUR WHOLE AFTERNOON.

A VARIETY OF SPECIALTY FEET ARE AVAILABLE FOR MOST MACHINE BRANDS. THEY AID THE SEWER IN PRODUCING MORE PROFESSIONAL-LOOKING RESULTS WITH LESS WORK AND TIME. MOST ACCESSORIES HAVE MULTIPLE USES AND WILL HELP YOU EXPAND YOUR SEWING HORIZONS.

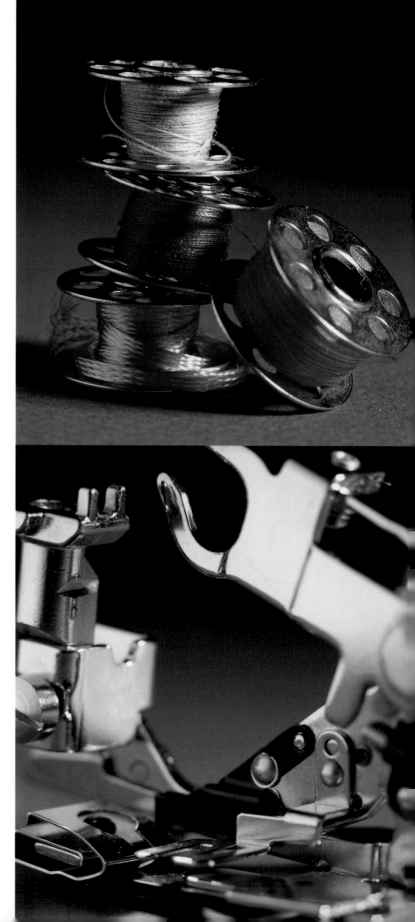

PINTUCKING

Materials:

- Fabric
- Pintuck foot (3-9 groove depending on fabric)
- Twin needle (1-4 mm depending on pintuck foot)
- 2 spools - cotton embroidery thread
- Gimp cord (optional)

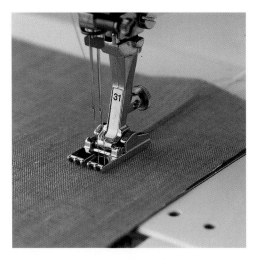

1. Refer to your sewing machine instruction manual for the set up for pintucking on your machine. Some machines add attachments while others add gimp cord to create the ridge or pintuck on the fabric.
2. Insert a double needle and thread the machine with two spools of embroidery thread. Insert one thread on either side of the upper tension disc and leave one thread out of the bottom tension guide by the needle. Make sure the threads do not cross each other. Insert the bobbin case and bring up the lower thread.
3. Attach the pintuck foot and using a straight stitch, length of $1\frac{1}{2}$ to $2\frac{1}{2}$ mm, pintuck the first row.

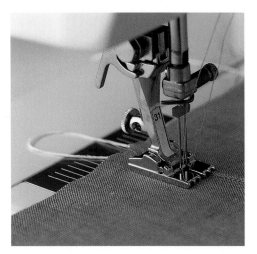

4. Turning at the end of a row of pintucks is made easier by releasing enough upper and lower thread to turn and start again.

5. Narrow spacing between pintucks can be achieved by placing a previously stitched row under one of the outer grooves of the pintuck foot. The presser foot groove will hold the stitched pintuck in place and the spacing between pintucks will remain even.

HEMSTITCHING

Materials:

- Crisp, lightweight, closely, woven natural fabric (such as cotton, organdy, linen, organza)
- Open embroidery foot
- Wing needle (120/19)
- Cotton or rayon embroidery thread
- Press cloth
- Spray-on fabric stabilizer or spray starch
- Chalk marker

1. Apply spray-on stabilizer to the fabric. Press the fabric using a press cloth and dry iron.
2. With the chalk marker, draw the first stitching line. **Note:** Stitching done on the bias or crosswise grain will result in more defined holes.
3. Stitch a line of triple zig-zag stitches using width of 3 mm and length of 2½ mm. Stitch slowly following the chalk line. If your machine has a half speed adjustment it may be used for better control.

4. Beginning at the same edge of the fabric, stitch a second row of triple zig-zag stitches to the right of the first row. The left holes of the second row of stitching should match exactly with the right holes of the first row of zig-zag stitches. Continue stitching rows as desired.

5. Once the stitching is completed, remove the stabilizer.

6. Other decorative and utility stitches may also be used for hemstitching, such as the versatile blindhem or vari-overlock stitch.

BOBBINWORK

Materials:

- Tightly woven fabric
- Extra bobbin case
- Cotton embroidery thread
- Decorative thread (such as ribbon floss or yarn)
- Tear-Away™ stabilizer

1. Hand wind the decorative thread onto a bobbin. Adjust the tension on the extra bobbin case so that the thread pulls freely under the tension spring.

2. Insert the bobbin case into the machine. Thread the machine with embroidery thread and tighten the needle tension. Pull the bobbin decorative thread to the top.

3. With the right side of the tightly woven fabric down, place the stabilizer or a second layer of fabric on top. Stitch using a long straight stitch, length of 4 mm, or choose a simple decorative stitch.

COUCHING

Materials:

- Fabric
- Braiding or cording foot
- Decorative thread (such as pearl cotton, soutache, yarn, metallic, rayon, rattail, ribbon floss)
- Tear-Away™ stabilizer (optional)
- Chalk marker
- Tapestry needle (optional)

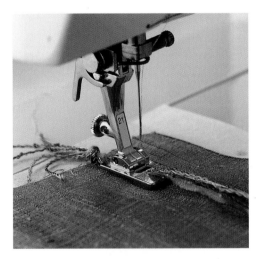

1. Draw a stitching line on the fabric with the chalk marker.
2. Thread the machine on the top and bottom with matching thread, decorative thread or use monofilament, if you don't want the stitches to show.
3. With right side up, layer the decorative fabric over the stabilizer. Place the layers under the presser foot. Knot the ends of the threads together if using multiple threads. Insert the decorative threads through the opening in the braiding foot and pull to the back.

4. Stitch over the threads following the marked stitching lines, creating a decorative trim. A zig-zag, blindhem or overlock stitch can be used. The stitch width must be wide enough to cover the threads. If using a single flat cord, attach it with a straight stitch.

5. Remove the stabilizer. If the threads are not enclosed in a seam, they can be pulled to the wrong side of the fabric with a tapestry needle and knotted. Couched threads can also be finished with a satin stitch, leaving the thread ends dangling for added embellishment.

RUFFLING

Materials:

- Ribbon or fabric
- Ruffler attachment
- Thread

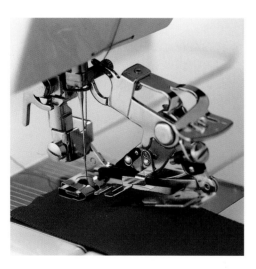

1. Attach the ruffler to the sewing machine and adjust the lever to gather the fabric as often as desired. Gathering every one to six stitches will produce the best results. Adjust the second gauge for the width of pleats desired (S=short, L=long). The needle position should be in the center with a stitch length of approximately 2.5mm.
2. To determine the exact amount of ribbon or fabric needed for each project, stitch samples using 12" pieces of ribbon or fabric. Then measure the fabric take up. Determine the ratio of fabric to the finished length needed.
3. Place the desired length of ribbon or fabric between the blades of the ruffler and pull slightly behind needle.

4. Lower the ruffler attachment and stitch.

PIPING

Materials:

- Fabric
- Fabric for piping
- Piping foot
- Rattail cord
- Chalk marker
- Ruler
- Rotary cutter and mat

1. Mark 2″ true bias strips on your fabric with a chalk marker and cut using a ruler and rotary cutter. True bias can be determined by folding a piece of fabric that has been cut on the straight of grain diagonally. Bias strips should be cut parallel to this diagonal fold.

2. If necessary, the bias strips may be joined together to form longer lengths. With right sides together, stitch the short ends of the strips together with a $\frac{1}{4}''$ seam.

3. With the right side of the fabric facing out, fold the bias strip around the rattail cord .
4. Attach the piping foot to the machine. Insert the filled bias strip under the foot so that the fabric and cord is guided through the center of the foot. Stitch with the needle in a far right or left position creating the piping.

5. Trim the seam allowance of the piping to the desired width.
6. With raw edges even, pin the piping to the base fabric. With the needle in a far right or far left position, stitch the piping to the fabric. Clip the piping seam allowance at corners and around curves so that the piping lies flat.

7. To finish, overlap the ends of the piping and stop stitching ½" from either side of the overlap.

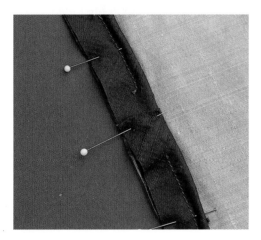

8. Remove the piping stitches on each of the overlapping ends. Cut the rattail cord so that the ends butt together. Place one end of the bias strip inside the other. Fold back the raw end of the outer bias strip ¼".
9. Finish stitching the piping to the fabric.
10. When stitching the piped fabric to the backing fabric, place right sides together, and stitch the edges with the needle in half right or half left position covering the previous row of stitching

SERGER EDGE FINISHES
FISHLINE EDGE

Materials:

- Fine fabric (such as batiste, organdy, fine cotton)
- Cording foot for serger
- 15 lb fishing line
- Woolly™ nylon thread
- 2 cones polyester thread

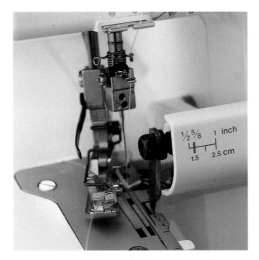

1. Attach the cording foot to the serger. Set the serger for a 3-thread rolled hem using Woolly™ nylon in the upper looper and polyester thread in the lower looper and needle. Adjust the stitch length and width to 1-1.5mm. Set the differential feed to 0.7mm.

2. Guide the fishing line under the cording foot following manufacturer's instructions. Pull about 4″ of fishing line through to the back of the foot.

3. Insert the fabric under the foot and serge the cord to the fabric edge, cutting off approximately a ¼″ of fabric. Loosely guide the cord while serging.

WIRE EDGED RIBBON

Materials:

- Firmly woven fabric (such as taffeta, organza, chintz, moiré)
- Cording foot for serger
- Rayon thread
- 2 cones polyester thread
- 28-30 gauge steel wire (fine fabrics) or 24-gauge steel wire (medium weight fabrics)
- Utility scissors
- Chalk marker

1. Attach the cording foot to the serger. Set the serger for a 3-thread rolled hem using rayon thread in the upper looper and polyester thread in the lower looper and needle. **Note:** Two strands of rayon thread may be used in the upper looper for additional coverage. Adjust the stitch length and width to 1-1.5mm. Set the differential feed to 0.7mm.
2. Cut the fabric into strips on either the lengthwise or crosswise grain, $1/2$" wider than the desired finished width. Using a chalk marker, draw lines $1/4$" inside the long edges of the fabric strips.

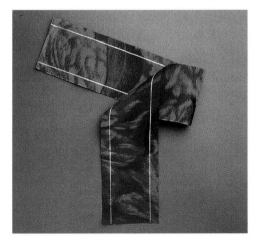

3. Guide the wire under the presser foot, pulling about 4" through to the back.
4. Insert the fabric strip under the foot and serge the wire to the fabric edge, aligning the needle with the chalk lines and cutting off $1/4$" from the edge. Trim off any extra wire with utility scissors when finished.
5. Insert the other edge of the fabric strip under the foot and serge the wire to the fabric in the same manner.

CHAPTER 3
BEAUTIFUL THINGS FROM THE PAST

IKE TREASURES FROM YOUR GRAND-MOTHER'S HOUSE, SACHETS CAN RECREATE THE PAST. DECORATIVE, SCENTED SHOE STUFFERS WERE USED TO PRESERVE A WOMAN'S FOOT FINERY IN THE 19TH CENTURY AND LAVENDER PACKAGES WERE PLACED ON HANGERS TO PERFUME WARDROBES. LADIES ADORNED THEIR DRESSERS WITH SACHETS EMBELLISHED WITH RIBBONS AND BEADS. NO SURFACE IN THE VICTORIAN HOME WAS LEFT BARE, EVEN DOOR KNOBS WERE FITTED WITH HANGING SACHETS.

SPECIAL OCCASIONS WERE CELEBRATED WITH SCENT. WEDDING SACHETS MADE OUT OF BRIDAL GOWN FABRIC AND LACE WERE GIVEN TO BRIDES AS A KEEPSAKE. DREAM PILLOWS WERE PRESENTED TO NEW MOTHERS WITH THE HOPE OF CAPTURING A FEW HOURS OF MUCH NEEDED REST. RECREATE A LITTLE VICTORIAN CULTURE FOR YOURSELF WHILE ALSO CREATING YOUR VERY OWN FAMILY HEIRLOOM.

CRINKLE BAG

Materials:

- 12″ x 5¹/₂″ of crinkled silk organza
- 5¹/₂″ of ³/₄″-1″ wide decorative trim
- ³/₄ yard of 1¹/₂″ wide wire-edged ribbon
- 6 faceted beads
- 3 gold seed beads
- 3 - ³/₈″ oval glass beads
- Beading needle
- Polyester thread
- Potpourri

1. Fold the fabric rectangle in half lengthwise. With right sides together, stitch the long side of the fabric together with a ³/₈″ seam forming a tube.
2. Fold the tube in half over itself with seams on the inside.
3. Sandwich the trim piece between the two inside raw edges stretching the fabric tube as needed. The flat edge of the trim piece and four raw edges of fabric should all be even. Pin all five layers together and stitch with a ¼″ seam.

4. Trim the corners. Turn the tube right side out.
5. Make a knot in a length of polyester thread and thread on the beading needle. Knot the thread to the trim at the center of the bag and thread on one faceted bead, one large oval bead, another faceted bead, and one gold seed bead. Pass the needle back up the second faceted bead, the large oval bead and the first faceted bead. Pull the thread taut aligning the beads and knot the thread to the trim.

6. Repeat the beading process at either end of the bag.
7. Fill the sachet bag half full with potpourri and tie the wire ribbon in a bow around the bag. Scrunch the bow for an antique effect.

SWEET ROLL

Materials:

- 4" x 12" rectangle of silk douppioni
- 1 yard ribbon floss
- $\frac{1}{2}$ yard of $\frac{1}{2}$" wide sheer ribbon
- 2 small silk roses with wire stems
- 2 small rubber bands
- Finely ground potpourri, lavender, or scented orrisroot

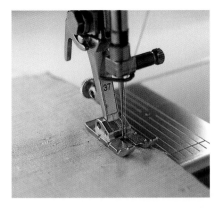

1. With right sides together, fold the rectangle in half and stitch a ¼" seam at both long edges.

2. Turn to the right side. Fill with a small amount of finely ground potpourri, lavender or scented orrisroot. Pin the bag opening closed and distribute the potpourri evenly in bag. To check if the potpourri amount is correct, roll the short ends of the bag to the center. Roll should be approximately 1½" in diameter. Adjust the amount of potpourri if necessary.
3. Serge or zig-zag the open end of the bag. Fold over ½" on each short end of the bag and pin in place.

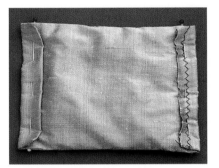

4. Roll the pinned ends of the bag to meet each other in the center. Secure in place with a rubber band. Remove the pins.

5. Secure at the center and either end by wrapping around the roll twice with heavy thread or ribbon floss and knotting on the back side of the roll where the ends are tucked in.
6. Twist the wire stems of the silk flowers around the center thread. Wrap the sheer ribbon around the center of the roll and tie in a bow between the flowers.

ENVELOPE WRAP

Materials:

- 2 - 6" x 8" rectangles of silk charmeuse
- 1 - 13" x 18" rectangle of organza
- 1 small frog closure
- Embroidery thread
- ¼" or Quilting foot
- Pattern "A"
- Potpourri

1. With right sides together, stitch the silk charmeuse rectangles together with a ½" seam, leaving a 2" opening for turning.
2. Trim and turn to the right side. Fill the bag with potpourri. (Bag should not be so full that it plumps up and no longer lays flat.) Slipstitch the opening closed.

3. Cut one piece out of organza from pattern "A". Using embroidery thread, stitch ¼" away from the outside edge. Trim the points off.

4. Press a ¼" seam allowance to the wrong side of the fabric using the stitching as a guide.
5. Fold again another ¼" enclosing the raw edge and press. On the right side of the fabric, stitch the fold in place ¼" away from the edge.

6. Handstitch the ends of the frog to the opposite corners of the right side of the organza fabric.

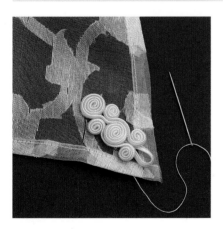

7. With the wrong side of the organza diamond facing up, place the charmeuse bag in the center of the fabric. Fold the edges without the frogs over the bag and pin together in the center. Hand stitch the ends in place.
8. Fold the remaining edges over the bag and fasten the frog closure.

SILVER TUFFET

Materials:

- 2 - 1$\frac{1}{2}$" decorative buttons
- 1 - 19" x 7$\frac{1}{2}$" rectangle of embroidered metallic organza
- Gimp cord
- Embroidery foot
- Polyester thread
- Potpourri

1. With right sides together, fold the fabric in half and stitch the short ends together with a $\frac{1}{2}''$ seam leaving a 2" opening to insert potpourri.

2. Press the seam open. With wrong sides together, fold the fabric tube in half lengthwise.
3. Pin the raw edges together. Thread gimp through the opening in the embroidery foot, and zig-zag over gimp, stitching $\frac{1}{4}''$ from the raw edge.

4. Pull the ends of the gimp cord gathering inside the edge of the tube tightly together. Knot the ends of gimp together and trim.
5. Fill the tuffet with potpourri and slipstitch the opening closed.
6. Using polyester thread, stitch the backside of the buttons together through the center, covering the gathered center edge.

LACED LADY

Materials:

- 16" of ⁵⁄₈" wide trim
- 2 - 6¹⁄₂" x 8" rectangles of silk
- 2 - 6" x 8" rectangle of silk
- 1 yard metallic cording of ¹⁄₄" ribbon
- Chalk marker
- Pinking shears
- Eyelet template
- Potpourri

1. Draw a line on the right side of both 6¹⁄₂" x 8" rectangles, 4" away from the left 8" edge. Pink the right 8" edge of rectangle.

2. With wrong sides together, fold along the line and press in place.
3. Draw another line 2" away from the left unfolded edge.

4. With right sides together, bring the folded edge to match up with the line. Press in place.

5. Topstitch the fold in place.

6. Repeat the process with the other 6½″ x 8″ rectangle.
7. Cut the trim piece in half. Pin the trim pieces to the rectangles, lining up against the topstitched fold. Stitch the trim in place.

8. Use the template to mark the placement of eyelets on the folded edge of rectangles. Stitch eyelets according to your machine's instructions.

9. Lace the cording through eyelets joining the rectangles and tie the ends in a bow. Knot the ends of the cord and fray. Pin one right side of one 6″ x 8″ rectangle to the wrong side of the laced fabric. Baste the layers together with a ¼″ seam.

10. With right sides together, stitch the remaining 6″ x 8″ rectangle to the laced fabric with a ³⁄₈″ seam, leaving a 2″ opening for turning.

11. Trim and turn to the right side. Fill with potpourri and slipstitch the opening closed.

CLOSET SACHET

Materials:

- 1 - 7″ square silk douppioni
- 1 - 4″ x 5″ rectangle silk douppioni
- ½ yard of 1½″ wide bias strip of silk douppioni
- 5″ of ½″ wide ribbon
- ½ yard rattail
- Rayon embroidery thread for monogram
- Stabilizer
- Piping foot
- Potpourri

1. Using an embroidery machine, center the monogram and border on the 7" square silk of douppioni with stabilizer underneath.
2. Trim the 7" square down to a 4" x 5" lengthwise rectangle with the monogram centered on the fabric.
3. Following directions for making piping in Chapter II, stitch piping to monogrammed rectangle, $\frac{1}{2}$" from outside edge.

4. Pin the ends of $\frac{1}{2}$" wide ribbon even with the raw edge of the top of the monogrammed rectangle. Ends are 1" apart. Baste in place.
5. With right sides together, stitch the fabric rectangles together with a $\frac{1}{2}$" seam. Use a piping foot and move the needle to half right. Leave a 2" opening at the bottom for turning.
6. Trim and turn to the right side. Fill with potpourri and slipstitch closed.
7. Place on a hanger.

WEDDING DAY

Materials:

- 32" of 5" wide lace trim
- 2 - 7½" squares of silk douppioni
- 11" square of silk charmeuse
- 6" square of crinoline
- ¼" pearl bead
- Polyester thread
- Cotton embroidery thread
- Open embroidery foot
- Potpourri

1. With the right side facing up, approximately 8" away from the left end of the trim piece (this will vary according to repeat of trim), fold the trim to form a 90° angle. Pin in place.

2. Using a small zig-zag stitch, 1½mm wide and 1mm long, and embroidery thread, stitch the miter in place. Trim the seam allowance close to the stitching.

3. Approximately 3″ away from the first miter, fold the lace again in the opposite direction of the first miter forming another 90° angle. Pin the fold and stitch in place with a narrow zig-zag. Trim the seam allowance.

4. Approximately 3″ away from the second miter, fold the lace again in the opposite direction, forming another 90° angle. Pin the miter and stitch in place with a narrow zig-zag. Trim the seam allowance.

5. Approximately 3″ away from the third miter, fold the end of the lace forming the last miter of the square. Pin the miter and stitch in place with a narrow zig-zag. Trim seam the allowance.

6. Center the wrong side of the lace on the right side of one silk douppioni square. Pin in place.

7. Stitch the inner edges of the lace square to the douppioni using embroidery thread.

8. Pin the edges of lace to the center of the square so they will not get caught in the bag construction.

9. With right sides together, stitch the silk douppioni squares together with a ¹/₂″ seam, leaving a 2″ opening for turning.

10. Trim and turn to right side. Fill with potpourri. Slipstitch opening closed.

The Flower

11. With right sides together, fold the 11″ square of silk in half, diagonally.

12. Hand sew ¹/₂″ long running stitches along the edge of the fold, leaving a thread tail.

13. Hand sew ¹/₂″ long running stitches along one double layer side of the triangle, close to the edge. Leave a thread tail at the same point as the previous stitching.

14. Pin the point of the fabric with the thread tails to the center of the crinoline square. Gather the running stitches and knot the thread tails together. Trim the thread. Turn the fabric right side out. Arrange the flower on the crinoline. Steam and press lightly with iron to set folds. Trim the extra crinoline away so that none shows on the right side.

15. Sew the pearl bead to the center of the flower.

16. Hand sew the crinoline with the flower to the center of the sachet.

DREAM PILLOW

Materials:

- 11¹⁄₂″ x 13³⁄₄″ striped silk douppioni (stripe runs parallel with 11¹⁄₂″ edge)
- 2 - 7″ x 9″ rectangles silk organza
- 13³⁄₄″ of ⁷⁄₈″ wide satin ribbon
- 12³⁄₄″ of 1″ wide decorative trim
- 2 - ¹⁄₄″ decorative beads
- 10″ of ¹⁄₄″ wide satin ribbon
- Large eye needle
- Edgestitch foot
- Fray Stop™
- Beading needle
- Polyester thread
- Potpourri (which contains lavender, chamomile, and rosemary to induce sleep)

The Pillowcase

1. On the right side of the striped fabric, place the satin ribbon $3\frac{1}{2}''$ away from one $13\frac{3}{4}''$ edge and machine baste in place through the center of the ribbon.
2. With wrong sides together, fold the striped rectangle in half matching the $11\frac{1}{2}''$ edges. Stitch the edges together with a $\frac{1}{4}''$ seam.

3. Turn to the wrong side. Press. With right sides together, stitch a $\frac{3}{8}''$ seam enclosing the raw edges in the seam.
4. Turn right side out. Press. With wrong sides together, stitch a $\frac{1}{4}''$ seam in the short end of the bag opposite the ribbon.
5. Turn to wrong side. Press. With right sides together, stitch a $\frac{3}{8}''$ seam enclosing the raw edges in the seam.
6. With wrong sides together, fold back the open end $\frac{1}{2}''$. Fold again $1\frac{1}{2}''$ and edgestitch the hem into place.
7. Apply Fray Stop™ to the ends of the decorative trim. Place the trim on top of the ribbon and stitch in place through the center of the trim.
8. Using a beading needle and polyester thread, sew $\frac{1}{4}''$ beads to the center of the trim, one on each side of the bag.

The Pillow

9. With right sides together, stitch the organza rectangles together with a $\frac{1}{2}''$ seam leaving a 2" opening for turning.
10. Trim and turn to the right side. Fill with potpourri and slipstich the opening closed.
11. Cut the $\frac{1}{4}''$ wide ribbon in half. Using a large eye needle, insert one piece of the ribbon $2\frac{1}{2}''$ from one short end of the potpourri bag. Sew from the top to bottom and back to the top. Tie in a bow. Repeat the process with the remaining ribbon $2\frac{1}{2}''$ away from the opposite end of the bag.

HANGING SACHET

Materials:

- 11" of ⅝" wide decorative trim
- 10" square of crinkled metallic silk organza
- 24" metallic gimp cord
- 2 metallic tassels on appox 19" cord
- 6 - ¼" diameter decorative beads.
- 12 sead beads
- Beading needle
- Edgestitch foot
- Polyester thread
- Potpourri

1. Using a narrow zig-zag, 2mm wide and 2mm long, stitch along the crosswise grain, ¼" away from each cut edge of the crinkled organza. Trim close to the stitching.

2. Pin the trim to the center of the right side of the crinkle fabric with cut ends of trim even with the unfinished edges of the fabric. Stretch the fabric as necessary. Edgestitch the trim in place.

3. With right sides together, stitch the unfinished edges of the crinkle fabric together with a $1/2$" seam.
4. Cut gimp in half and fold one piece in half again. Place the cut ends 2" inside the top end of the tube. Using the free arm of the sewing machine, stitch the ends in place to a single layer of fabric.

5. Tightly tie the cording with tassels into a knot 2" from the bottom end the of the tube. Then tie a bow around the fabric, closing the bottom end of the tube.

6. Fill the bag with potpourri to within 2" of the top. Tightly tie the remaining piece of gimp cord in a knot 2" inside the top end and then tie a bow around the fabric closing the bag opening.
7. Using a beading needle and polyester thread, stitch the beads to the bottom end of the trim, as shown, spacing evenly around the sachet.

SCENTED SHOE STUFFERS

Materials:

- $\frac{1}{2}$ yard of $\frac{1}{2}$" wide trim
- $\frac{1}{2}$ yard of $\frac{1}{4}$" diameter cording
- $\frac{3}{8}$ yard of fine linen
- Polyester fiberfill stuffing
- #120 wing needle
- Cotton embroidery thread
- Pattern "B" & "C"
- $\frac{1}{4}$" or Quilting foot
- Spray fabric stabilizer or starch
- 2 tablespoons scented orrisroot

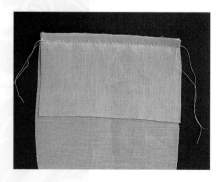

1. Cut four pieces of pattern "B" and four pieces of pattern "C" out of linen fabric.
2. Cut $\frac{1}{2}$" wide trim into four $4\frac{1}{4}$" pieces.
3. With right sides together, line up the straight edge of the trim with the top edge of "B". Baste in place.
4. With right sides together, match up "C" and "B" along the top edge. Stitch the top edges together with a $\frac{1}{4}$" seam.

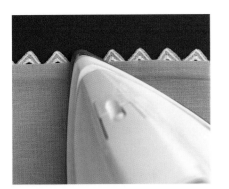

5. Press "C" and "B" away from the trim. Spray fabric stabilizer on all four pieces following the manufacturers instructions.

6. Using a wing needle and embroidery thread, stitch the two rows of hemstitching on all four pieces through both layers, starting $3/8$" away from the trim and running parallel to the trim. See Hemstitching in Chapter II.

7. Remove the fabric stabliizer.
8. With right sides together, stitch each pair of "B's" together along the rounded edges with a $1/4$" seam.

9. Turn to the right side. Place a line of stitching $1\,3/8$" inside the top edge of the bag through all layers, leaving a $1\,1/2$" opening at one end.
10. Fill the bags firmly with polyester fiberfill and one tablespoon of scented orrisroot.
11. Complete the stitching to close the bag. Cut the cording into two 9" pieces and tie around the top of stuffers, covering the line of stitching.

HALF AND HALF

Materials:

- 2 - 7″ squares of coordinating silk
- 32″ of ⅝″ wide trim
- Walking foot
- Chalk marker
- Potpourri

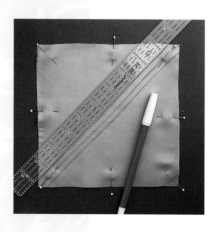

1. With right sides together, pin the squares to one another. Draw a line with the chalk marker diagonally across the squares. Draw lines ¼″ away on either side of the center diagonal line.

2. Using a walking foot, stitch through both layers along the two outer lines. Cut the square apart at the center diagonal line.

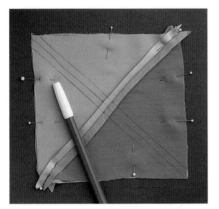

3. Press the seams open.
4. Pin the squares, right sides together and opposite colors of the triangles facing each other. Draw a diagonal line with chalk across the squares perpendicular to the previous seam. Draw an additional line $1/4''$ away on either side of the diagonal line.
5. Using a walking foot, stitch along the two outer lines. Cut the square apart at the center diagonal line. Press the seams open and trim the squares to 6″.

6. Cut the trim into four pieces. Center the pieces of trim over the diagonal seams on the fabric squares and stitch in place.
7. Place the squares, right sides together, and trim the pieces on top of each other and opposite colors of the triangles facing one another. Stitch together with a $1/4''$ seam leaving a 2″ opening for turning.
8. Trim and turn to the right side. Fill with potpourri and slipstitch the opening closed.

ORGANZA MERINGUE

Materials:

- 2 - 5¹/₂″ squares silk satin
- 1 - 19″ diameter circle of silk organza
- ³/₄ yard of 1¹/₂″ wide varigated wire-edged ribbon
- Purchased fabric flowers
- Woolly™ nylon serger thread
- 15 lb fishing line
- Fray Stop™
- Serger cording foot
- Potpourri

1. With right sides together, stitch the satin squares together using a ¹/₄″ seam, leaving a 2″ opening for turning.
2. Trim and turn to the right side. Fill with potpourri and slipstitch the opening closed.

3. Using the cording foot, serge the fishing line to the outside edge of the organza circle. Overlap the ends of serging and apply Fray Stop™ before trimming. See Serger Corded Edges in Chapter II.
4. Place the satin bag in the center of the circle. Gather the organza around the satin bag with the wire-edged ribbon. Tie the ribbon in a bow and insert the fabric flower stems into the center of the bow. Trim the ends of the ribbon into a "V".

CHAPTER 4

RIBBON FANTASIES

IBBONS ARE A WONDERFUL EMBEL-
LISHMENT FOR ANY SEWING PROJECT.
THEY CAN TAKE AN ITEM FROM THE
MUNDANE TO THE EXCEPTIONAL. RIBBON ART BECAME
POPULAR DURING THE 1920'S. FLAPPER DRESSES, HATS
AND HANDBAGS WERE ADORNED WITH RIBBON
FLOWERS AND PLEATED COCARDS. THE MILLINERY
DEPARTMENT OF THE WOMAN'S INSTITUTE OF
DOMESTIC ARTS AND SCIENCES PRODUCED A
PUBLICATION CALLED, "*RIBBON TRIMMINGS, A COURSE
IN SIX PARTS*" AS A TEXTBOOK OF TECHNIQUES.
RECENTLY REPRINTED BY VIV'S RIBBON & LACE, IT IS AN
EXCELLENT RESOURCE GUIDE FOR THE LOVER OF
RIBBON ART.

CANDACE KLING, A SAN FRANCISCO ARTIST, IS
TODAY'S MASTER OF RIBBON WORK. SHE HAS STUDIED
VINTAGE GARMENTS AND LADIES PUBLICATIONS IN HER
PURSUIT OF KNOWLEDGE OF RIBBON WORK. MANY OF
THE TECHNIQUES IN THIS CHAPTER WERE LEARNED
FROM CANDACE. I HOPE THEY WILL ALSO INSPIRE
YOU TO LEARN MORE.

RIBBON COCARD

Materials:

- 42" of 1½" wide plaid ribbon
- 4" square crinoline
- 2 - 6" squares silk douppioni
- 2 - 7" squares silk douppioni
- 1 yard of ⅝" wide ribbon
- Topstitching thread
- Hand needle
- 1 - 1" decorative button
- Potpourri

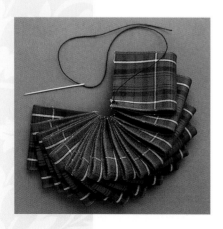

1. Cut the 1½" wide ribbon into fourteen 3" pieces. With wrong sides together, fold the ribbon pieces in half and string them with a hand needle onto knotted topstitching thread, piercing the unfolded corner, ⅛" inside the top raw edges and right finished edge.

2. Allow 1" of the thread between the first strung piece and the last. Knot the thread after the last piece.

3. Join the knots at the beginning and the end to form a circle. Trim the thread.

4. Place the ribbon in the center of the crinoline with raw edges down. Flatten out the ribbon circle. Arrange the folded edges to lay on the outside of the circle in the same direction and of equal distance from each other. Pin the ribbon raw edges in place in the center.

5. At the center of the cocard, stitch each petal to the crinoline. Trim away any extra crinoline so none shows from the top. Stitch the button to the center of the cocard.

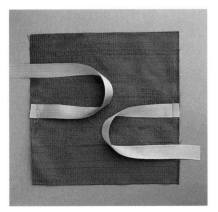

6. Cut the ⅝″ ribbon into four ¼ yard pieces.

7. Pin one piece of the ribbon to the right side of one 6″ square of silk, raw edges even and centering the ribbon. Baste in place ¼″ from the edge.

8. Repeat the process with another piece of ribbon on the opposite edge.

9. Repeat the process on one 7″ square attaching the ribbons to the center of the opposite sides.

10. Pin the ribbons to the center of the squares so they will not get caught in the construction stitching. With right sides together, stitch the 6″ squares with a ½″ seam leaving a 2″ opening for turning.

11. Trim and turn to the right side. Remove the pins and trim the ribbon ends in a "V".

12. Repeat the process with the 7″ square.

13. Fill the bags with potpourri and slipstitch the opening closed.

14. Stitch the crinoline with the cocard to the top of the small bag.

15. Place the small bag on top of the large bag, aligning the sides with the ribbons. Tie the ribbons into a bow on each side.

RUFFLED FLOWER

Materials:

- 2 yards of 1¹/₂″ wide silk ribbon
- 2 - 5″ diameter linen circles
- 1 - 15¹/₂″ x 2¹/₂″ rectangle of linen
- 1 - 1⁵/₈″ diameter button
- Ruffler attachment
- Potpourri

1. Cut the ribbon into a ¹/₂ yard piece and a 1¹/₂ yard piece. Using the ruffler attachment, make small ruffles in the ribbons ¹/₂″ away from one lengthwise edge. Ruffle or gather each piece of ribbon. See instructions for Ruffling in Chapter II.
2. With right sides together, stitch the cut ends of the ¹/₂ yard ruffled ribbon piece together with a ¹/₄″ seam.

3. When opened up and laid flat, the ribbon should form approximately a 3½" diameter circle.

4. Repeat the process with the 1½ yard piece of ruffled ribbon to form approximately a 4½" diameter circle.
5. Center the larger ribbon circle on the right side of one linen circle. Pin the ribbon in place and stitch to the fabric using the previous ruffle stitching as a guide.
6. Center the small ribbon circle on top of the larger ribbon circle. Pin in place and stitch to the fabric.

7. Handstitch a button to the center of the linen circle covering the ribbon edges and stitching lines.
8. Staystitch ³⁄₈" along both long edges of the linen rectangle. Clip every ³⁄₄".
9. With right sides together, stitch the short ends of the linen rectangle together with a ½" seam. Press the seam open.
10. Pin the ribbon ruffles together in the center to prevent them from being caught in the stitching. With right side together, pin the linen rectangle to the outside edge of the circle keeping raw edges even. Stitch together with a ½" seam.
11. Trim the seam and remove the pins from the ribbon. With right sides together, stitch the remaining linen circle to the other edge of the rectangle leaving a 2" opening for turning. Trim and turn to the right side. Fill with potpourri and slipstitch the opening closed.

WOVEN RIBBON HEART

Materials:

- 6" square of fusible interfacing
- Bodkin
- Ribbons for weaving:
  - ½ yard of 5 colors of ½"-⅝" ribbon or rayon seam tape
  - ½ yard of ¾" wide metallic ribbon
  - 12" of 1" wide decorative ribbons
- Padded ironing board or pin weaving board

- Pattern "D"
- ¼" or Quilting foot
- 12" of ⅝" ribbon or seam tape
- 7" square of silk
- 1 - 1" heart-shaped button
- Scented buckwheat

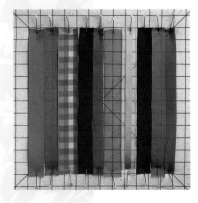

1. Cut all the ribbons for weaving into 6" pieces. Line up half of the ribbon pieces vertically on a padded ironing or pin weaving board arranging the colors and sizes as desired. **Note:** If the ribbon has a definite right and wrong side, place the right side facing down on the padded board. Pin the top ends in a straight line keeping the ribbons properly aligned. Pin the bottom ends of the ribbons in place. There should be no space in between ribbons.

2. Using a bodkin, weave the remaining ribbons horizontally through the vertical ribbons. Weave over the first ribbon, under the second, over the third and so on to the other side. The next ribbon will be woven under the first ribbon, over the second and under the third, and so on. Secure the horizontal ribbons with pins on both ends as you go.

3. When the weaving is finished, square the ribbons making sure there are no gaps between the ribbons and the ribbons are straight.
4. Remove all of the right horizontal pins. Lay a square of fusible interfacing over the ribbon with the fusible side down and press into place.

5. Remove the remaining pins. Stitch along the outside edge on all sides securing the ends of the ribbon. Center pattern "D" diagonally over the right side of the woven ribbon piece and cut out. Cut out a second heart from the solid square of silk.
6. Place the "D" sections, right sides together, and stitch with a $1/4$" seam leaving a 2" opening for turning.
7. Turn to the right side and fill with scented buckwheat. Slipstitch the opening closed.
8. Make a bow in the remaining 12" piece of ribbon and center on the heart near the top. Handstitch the bow to the heart and cut the ribbon ends into a "V". Stitch the heart-shaped button to the center of the bow.

SHEER OVERLAYS

Materials:

- 2 - 6" squares of silk douppioni
- 21" of 5″ or 6″ wide sheer gold ribbon
- 2 abalone buttons (1 - 1″ diameter, 1 - $^1/_2$″ diameter)
- 1 small bead
- Polyester thread
- Potpourri or Lavender

1. Cut the ribbon into two pieces. Fold each ribbon in half lengthwise and trim 1$^1/_2$" off each end and cut to a point.

2. Open the ribbon flat and machine baste each piece ¼" from the edge.

3. Align the point of one end of the ribbon to a corner on the right side of a 6" square. Pin in place. Gather the ribbon up to 2" on either side of the corner and baste in place ¼" from the raw edge.

4. Repeat on the opposite corner of the square with the other end of the ribbon. Wrap and gather the center of the ribbon overlay several times with polyester thread and tie in a knot.

5. Repeat the process with the second ribbon piece on the remaining corners, laying the ribbon over the previously stitched overlay. Wrap the center of the ribbon overlay several times with polyester thread and tie in a knot. Tie the upper and lower overlays together with thread and knot.

6. Sew the 1" and ½" buttons and bead to the center of the square on top of the overlays, stitching through the fabric and both overlays.

7. With right sides together, stitch the fabric square together with a ⅜", seam leaving a 2" opening for turning.

8. Turn to the right side. Fill with potpourri or lavender and slipstitch the opening closed.

BLOOMING COLORS

Materials:

- 1- 7″ and 1 - 6″ squares of silk douppioni
- 1½ yards of 1½″ wide ribbon
- ½″ covered button kit (4 finished buttons)
- 4 - ½″ two hole shirt buttons
- 4 - 2″ squares of coordinating fabric (for covered buttons)
- Polyester thread
- Ruffler attachment
- Edgestitch foot
- Chalk marker
- Scented orrisroot or buckwheat

1. On the wrong side of the 7″ fabric square, center and mark a diagonal line across the fabric with the chalk marker.
2. Mark additional parallel lines, 1½″ on either side of the first. Repeat, drawing lines 1½″ away from these lines.

3. Fold the fabric, right sides together, at the chalk lines and stitch ⅛″ away from folded edge using the edgestitch foot.

4. Press the seam to one side.
5. On the wrong side of the fabric, mark a diagonal line across the fabric perpendicular to the stitched tucks.

6. Repeat steps 2, 3 and 4. Square up the fabric edges if necessary.
7. Ruffle or gather the ribbon $^3/_8$" inside one lengthwise edge. See instructions for Ruffling in Chapter II. You will need approximately 24" of ruffled or gathered ribbon. Pink one raw edge of the ribbon and turn back $^1/_4$".
8. With right sides together, pin the ribbon to the tucked fabric square, starting with the folded end of ribbon facing up. The ruffled edge of the ribbon should be on the outside lined up with the raw edge of the fabric. The ruffles face the center.
9. Overlap the ends of the ribbon 1". Pink the raw edge of the top ribbon and turn back $^1/_4$" with the edge facing up.
10. With the ruffles facing up, stitch the ribbon to the fabric, $^1/_2$" from the raw edge, rounding the corner and stitching as necessary. Steam the ruffles to keep them in place, flattening slightly. Pin the ruffles down if necessary so they will not get caught in the stitching of the bag.

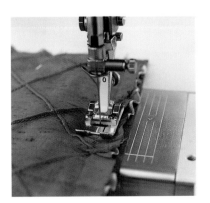

11. With right sides together and tucked side facing up, stitch the tucked fabric and plain fabric squares together $^1/_2$" from the raw edge using the previous stitching as a guide and leaving a 2" opening for turning.
12. Trim the seam allowance and turn to the right side. Fill with scented orrisroot or buckwheat. Slipstitch the opening closed.
13. Following button kit instructions, cover $^1/_2$" button forms with coordinating 2" fabric squares. Using polyester thread, stitch the covered buttons to the right side of the bag and shirt buttons to the wrong side of the bag where shown.

RIBBON CANDY

Materials:

- $\frac{1}{2}$ yard of $1\frac{1}{2}''$ wide picot edged ribbon
- 2 - 4" x $6\frac{1}{2}''$ squares of silk douppioni
- Silk pins
- 3 small beads
- Beading needle
- Polyester thread
- Potpourri

1. Make a ³/₄" pleat 3" from one end of the ribbon, facing the same end. Secure the pleat with a pin.
2. Next to the first pleat, make a second ³/₄" pleat in the opposite direction of the first. Pin in place.

3. Make four more pleats in the same order, pinning as you go.
4. Machine stitch through the center of the box pleats to secure in place.

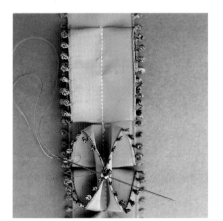

5. Handstitch the center of each pleat with polyester thread and secure with one bead.
6. With right sides together, stitch the fabric rectangles together with a ³/₈" seam leaving a 2" opening for turning.
7. Trim and turn to the right side. Fill with potpourri and slipstitch the opening closed.
8. Center the pleated ribbon lengthwise on the sachet and pin in place. Secure the ribbon to the bag with concealed hand stitches. Cut the ends of the ribbon even and trim into a "V".

BOUDOIR SACHET

Materials:

- 11″ of 2″ wide metallic ribbon
- 5½″ of 2″ wide sheer ribbon
- 12″ of ½″ wide metallic ribbon
- ⅝″ diameter wire mesh rose
- Hot glue gun
- Potpourri

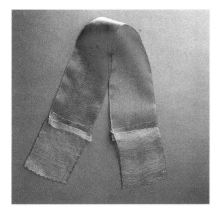

1. Cut the 5½″ piece of ribbon in half. Pink one end of each half. With right sides together, stitch the unpinked ends of the sheer ribbon to each end of the 11″ ribbon with a ¼″ seam allowance. Press the seam open.

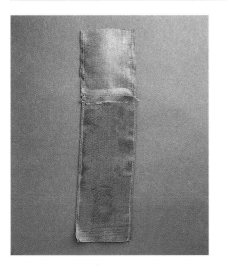

2. With right sides together, fold the ribbon in half matching the seams. Stitch the sides together with as small a seam allowance as possible.

3. Turn to the right side and fold the sheer ribbon to the inside leaving ½″ showing at the top. Fill with colorful potpourri.
4. Tie the ½″ metallic ribbon across the seam of the bag. Cut the ribbon ends into a "V" and wrap around a pencil. Steam the ends with an iron to curl.
6. Center the wire rose over the tied ribbon and hot glue into place.

LEAVES AND FLOWER BUDS

Materials:

- 9″ x 4½″ rectangle of velvet
- 14″ of 1″ wide variegated ribbon
- 12″ of ¼″ wide ribbon
- 16″ of 1½″ wide green ribbon
- 3″ square black crinoline
- Handful of polyester fiberfill
- Walking foot
- Scented orrisroot or buckwheat

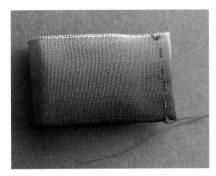

The Berry

1. Cut the 1″ variegated ribbon into 3¹/₂″ pieces.
2. To form the berries, fold the ribbon pieces in half with right sides together and handstitch the raw edges together with a ¹/₈″ seam.
3. Press the seam open with your fingers and turn right side out.

4. Handstitch a single layer on one edge of the tube with long gathering stitches, very close to the selvedge. This is the bottom of the berry. The color of the berry can be changed depending upon which side of the variegated ribbon you choose for the top.
5. Pull the gathering stitches and knot.

6. Handstitch through a single layer on the opposite edge of the tube with long gathering stitches, very close to the selvedge. The shape of the berry can be changed by stitching ¹/₄″ away from the finished edge.
7. Stuff with polyester fiberfill. Pull the gathering stitches closed and knot.

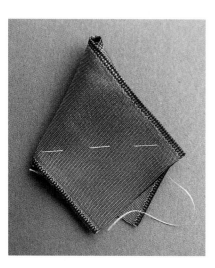

The Leaves

8. Cut the 1½″ green ribbon into 4″ pieces.

9. Fold one end of the ribbon across the center at a 45° angle.

10. Fold the other end of the ribbon at a 45° angle. Handstitch through all the layers as shown.

11. Pull the handstitches and wrap the thread around the ribbon to secure and knot. Trim the ends of the ribbon.

12. Arrange the leaves and buds on the crinoline and handstitch in place. Trim any extra crinoline away from the arrangement so none shows on top.

The Bag

13. With right sides together, fold the velvet rectangle in half and stitch together with a ¼″ seam and a walking foot, leaving a 2″ opening for turning.

14. Trim and turn to the right side. Fill the bag three-quarters full with scented orrisroot or buckwheat. Slipstitch the opening closed. Bring the opposite corners of the velvet square together in the center and handstitch.

15. Cut the ¼″ wide ribbon into a 7″ and a 5″ piece. Slide the ribbons under the gathered corners and handstitch in place.

16. Center the crinoline with the buds and leaves over the velvet bag and handstitch into place.

HORSEHAIR BAG

Materials:
- 1¼ yard of 5½″ wide horsehair braid
- 9″ of gimp cord
- 1 - 2″ two-hole button
- 1 - 3″ tassel
- Potpourri

1. With wrong sides together, fold up one cut end of horsehair 5½". Pin in place and stitch the finished edges together from the fold to the top with a ⅜" seam.

2. With wrong sides together, fold up the same end of the horsehair braid 12½" with the smaller bag opening on the inside. Pin in place and stitch the edges together with a ⅜" seam starting at the fold and ending 6½" inside. Keep the smaller bag free of the stitching.

3. With wrong sides together, fold up the same end of horsehair 15", keeping the smaller bags free of stitching. Pin in place and stitch the finished edges together with a ⅜" seam starting at the fold and ending 8" inside.

4. Trim off any extra horsehair braid above the last stitching. Fold the bags down in place, stacking on top of each other.

5. Fill the three bags half full with potpourri. Thread the gimp cord through the button. Tie the tassel to the top of the button. Tightly tie and knot the cording with the button 3" from the top of the bags, closing the opening.

CHAPTER 5

CONTEMPORARY INTERPRETATIONS

SCENTED PACKAGES TAKE ON A MORE CONTEMPORARY FLAIR BY INCORPORATING MACHINE TECHNIQUES WITH THE TRADITIONAL. EXPERIMENT WITH THE SPECIALTY ACCESSORIES AVAILABLE FOR YOUR MACHINE THAT COUCH THREADS AND STITCH PRECISE PINTUCKS. PLACE DECORATIVE THREAD ON THE BOBBIN AND FORM A NEW FABRIC WITH POCKETS.

THE SHAPE OF THE PACKAGE ITSELF CAN ADD A MODERN TWIST TO A SACHET. PLEATED CHARMEUSE BECOMES A BEAUTIFUL PEAR; BRIGHTLY COLORED SILK DOUPPIONI MAKES A SCENTED HOLIDAY ORNAMENT; OR SUBTLY COLORED ORGANZA IS FOLDED INTO AN ORIGAMI BOX TO HOLD WHOLE DRIED FLOWERS. TRADITIONAL IDEAS TURN INTO CONTEMPORARY TREASURES WITH THE INTRODUCTION OF NEW SHAPES, FABRICS AND SEWING TECHNIQUES.

HOLIDAY ORNAMENT

Materials:

- ¹⁄₈ yard of striped silk douppioni
- ¹⁄₈ yard of each of two colors of coordinating solid silk douppioni
- 8" of ³⁄₈" wide grosgrain ribbon
- 8 seed beads
- 2 oval glass beads

- Beading needle
- Polyester thread
- Pattern "E" and "G"
- Chalk marker
- Potpourri

1. Cut out striped douppioni using pattern "E". Cut out solid douppioni using pattern "G".
2. With right sides together, stitch pieces "G" together along the short, straight edge with a ¹⁄₄" seam. Press.

3. With right sides together, stitch "E" and "G" together with a ¹⁄₄" seam, leaving a small opening as indicated.

4. Trim the points, turn to the right side and press.
5. Fold in half at the seam on "G" with "E" on the inside. Stitch the sides together using a $\frac{1}{4}$" seam starting at the folded edge and stopping at the small dots.

6. Press the seam open and trim the corners at the fold.
7. Turn the bag right side out. Fold the cuff down over the body. The bag is now approximately $3\frac{1}{2}$" tall.

8. Fill two-thirds of the bag with potpourri. Fold the opening edge of the bag in half matching the side seams in the center.

9. Fold the ribbon in half and insert $\frac{1}{2}$" of the cut edges into the bag opening, lining up with the bag seam allowance. Pin the ribbon in place on the body of the bag only.
10. Pull the bag out straight and draw a line with chalk $3\frac{1}{2}$" away from the bottom of the bag. Stitch through all the layers along the chalk line, closing the opening and catching the ribbon as you stitch.

11. Fold the cuff down over the stitching. Attach the beads to the cuff points using polyester thread and a beading needle

BOBBINWORK BEAD POCKETS

Materials:

- 3 - 5¼" squares of metallic silk organza
- 1 spool ribbon floss
- 1 tablespoon mixed bugle beads, seed beads, sequins
- Extra bobbin case
- Stitching guide attachment (optional)
- Large eye needle
- Potpourri

1. Hand wind the ribbon floss onto a bobbin. Adjust the tension on the bobbin case so the ribbon floss pulls freely out of the case. Tighten the needle tension, if necessary, to achieve a more loopy stitch. See instructions for Bobbinwork in Chapter II.
2. Pin two squares of the organza together and straight stitch rows 1¼" apart and ¾" from each end, as shown, with the right side facing down. Use a stitching guide attachment, if available, to keep rows straight.

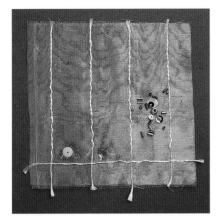

3. Rotate the fabric one quarter turn and stitch a row ³/₄″ away from the edge of the fabric.
4. Insert a pinch of beads into each stitched row between the layers of organza, pushing the beads down to meet the first row of stitching.

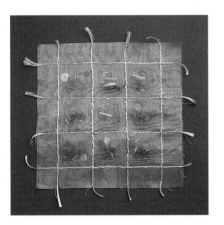

5. Stitch a second row 1¹/₄″ away from the first row of pockets. Repeat the process two more times forming six 1¹/₄″ pockets.

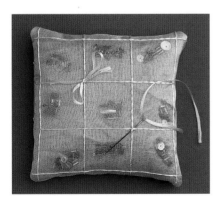

6. With right sides together, stitch the layer with pockets to the remaining organza square with a ¹/₄″ seam, leaving a 2″ opening for turning.
7. Turn to the right side. Fill with potpourri and slipstitch the opening closed.
8. Thread a strand of ribbon floss through two corners of stitching on top of the pillow using a large eye needle. Tie the floss in a bow.

PEAR

Materials:

- 1 - 14" x 6½" rectangle of silk charmeuse
- Fabric pleater
- 1 velvet leaf with wire stem
- 1 small twig
- Glue gun
- 1" square of felt
- Chalk marker
- Potpourri

1. With the fabric pleater openings facing away, start at the closest fold and with the right side of the fabric facing down, push the short end of the fabric into a fold. Use a stiff card to insert the fabric or just your fingers alone. Work the fabric up the pleater until it is all pushed into the folds.

2. Steam the fabric in the pleater with an iron and let it cool completely. Remove the fabric by rolling the pleater backwards. This causes the pleats to open.

3. With right sides together, stitch the 6$\frac{1}{2}$" ends of the fabric together with a $\frac{1}{4}$" seam.

4. Stitch a row of long basting stitches $\frac{1}{2}$" from each open end of the tube through a single layer of fabric.

5. Lay the tube flat and make a line with tailors chalk 3$\frac{1}{4}$" from one open end. Baste along the marked line through a single layer.

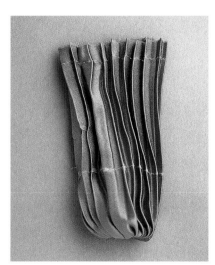

6. With right sides together, draw up the bottom row of basting stitches closing the tube of fabric. Knot the basting threads. Trim the ends and turn the bag right side out keeping the gathered seam allowance inside.

7. Fill with potpourri up to the center basting stitches. Gather the center basting stitches and knot the ends of the thread. Trim the thread ends.

8. Fill the top section of the pear with potpourri up to the top basting stitches. Gather the top basting stitches pushing the seam allowance to the inside and closing the tube of fabric. Knot the ends of the thread and trim.

9. Pink the edge of the felt piece into an oval shape and hot glue it to the bottom of the pear.

10. Hot glue the bottom of a small stick into top of pear for a stem. Insert the wire stem of a velvet leaf into top of the pear and hot glue the back of the leaf to the pear.

TUXEDO

Materials:

- 1 - 5³/₄" x 6" rectangle of fine linen or cotton shirting
- 1 - 5" x 5¹/₂" rectangle of fine linen or cotton shirting
- Pintucking foot
- 3 mm double needle
- 2 spools embroidery thread
- White gimp cord
- 5" of ³/₄" wide ribbon
- 3 small shirt buttons
- Potpourri or scented buckwheat

1. Stitch three rows of single pintucks ⁵/₈" away from the short end of the 5³/₄" x 6" rectangle of linen, with a ¹/₄" space between each row. See instructions for pintucking in Chapter II.

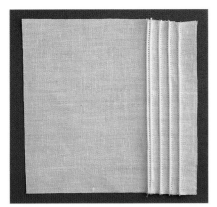

2. Stitch a double row of pintucks $1/4''$ away from the last single row of pintucks.

3. Stitch four single pintuck rows $1/4''$ away from the double row of pintucks with a $1/4''$ space between each row.

4. Stitch a double row of pintucks $1/4''$ away from the last single row of pintucks.

5. Stitch three single rows $1/4''$ away from the double row of pintucks with $1/4''$ space between each row.

6. Stitch a double row of pintucks in the center of the fabric perpendicular to the previously stitched pintucks.

7. Stitch a double row of pintucks $1^{1}/4''$ on either side of the center double row.

8. Handstitch buttons to the center of the rectangle at the double stitched horizontal rows of pintucks.

9. Trim the rectangle, if necessary, to $5'' \times 5^{1}/2''$.

10. With right sides together, stitch the pintucked fabric to plain backing fabric with a $3/8''$ seam leaving a $2''$ opening for turning.

11. Trim and turn to the right side. Fill with scented buckwheat or potpourri. Slipstitch the opening closed.

12. Pink the ends of the ribbon and fold the ends toward one another overlapping approximately 1" in center.

13. Handstitch through the center of the folded ribbon and gather. Wrap thread around the center to secure and knot. Place the "bowtie" at the center of one end of the sachet and stitch in

LAVENDER LINGERIE BAG

Materials:

- 2 - 13" metallic silk organza squares
- ¾ yard of metallic gimp cord
- 1 - 1½" eye pin
- 2 - decorative beads
- 1 seed bead
- Chalk marker
- 2" wide ruler
- Teaspoon
- Fray Stop™
- Needlenose pliers
- ¼" or Quilting foot
- Zipper foot
- Lavender

1. Press under ½" on one side of each organza square. Trim to ¼". With the folded edges to the outside, pin the organza squares together and stitch the non-folded edges together with a ½" seam.

2. Trim the seam allowance to $^1/_4''$. Turn to the right side and press. Baste the opening closed $^1/_4''$ from the folded edge.
3. Divide the square with chalk into six 2" sections perpendicular to basted end.

4. Stitch along the marked lines to form tubes. Remove the basting from the folded edge. Divide the tubes into six 2" squares perpendicular to the previous stitching lines. **Do not stitch yet.** Fill all six tubes with one teaspoon of lavender. Shake the lavender to the bottom of the tubes and stitch along the first chalk mark.
5. Repeat the process of filling and stitching the tubes four more times.

6. For the final sections, fill each tube with a teaspoon of lavender and pin the folded opening closed. Insert the gimp cord into one corner of the folded end and pin in place.
7. Topstitch the opening closed with a $^1/_8''$ seam.
8. Fold the square in half and stitch the folded edge without gimp cord together with a $^1/_8''$ seam.

9. Fold the square in half in the opposite direction and stitch the folded edge without gimp together with a $^1/_8''$ seam.
10. Turn the bag right side out.
11. Slide the seed bead and then two decorative beads onto an eye pin. Using pliers, bend the straight end of the eye pin into a loop.
12. Thread the end of the gimp cord through the top loop of the eye pin and knot the cord. Apply Fray Stop™ to the knot and when dry, trim the end of the gimp at the knot. Wrap the gimp around the bag.

MARCY'S ORIGAMI BOX

Materials:

- 1 - 14" square of organza
- 1 - 13⅝" square of organza
- Metallic thread
- Chalk marker
- Whole dried flowers and leaves

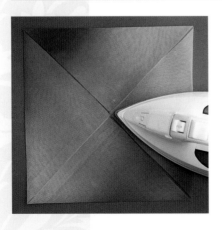

The Top

1. Mark the center of the 14" square with a chalk marker.
2. Fold four corners of the square to the center. Press

3. Fold the left and right sides to the center. Press.

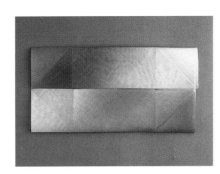

4. Unfold and fold the opposite sides to the center. Press.

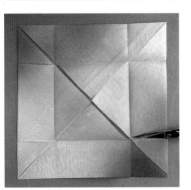

5. Unfold. Cut along the four foldlines as shown.

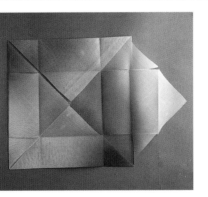

6. Unfold the right center section. Unfold the top and bottom triangles of the right section.

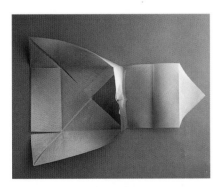

7. Bring the left and right triangles together and overlap one in front of the other. Pin in place.
8. Using matching polyester thread, secure the triangles together in the center with small hand stitches.
9. Fold the center flap over the joined section. Pin in place.
10. Repeat the process on the opposite side of the square.

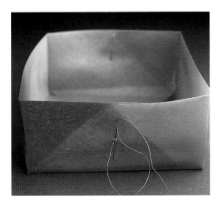

11. Using metallic thread, secure the two pinned sides with small handstitches.
12. Using metallic thread, handstitch the four corners in place in the center of the top.

The Bottom

13. Repeat all the steps with the $13^5/_8$" square.
14. Fill the bottom of the box with dried, whole flowers and leaves. Place the top on the box.

LINEN PILLOW TRIO

Materials:

- 6 - 6" squares of linen
- 1 yard of ⅝" wide satin ribbon
- 2 velvet leaves with wire stems
- 1 cinnamon stick
- Scented buckwheat

1. With right sides together, stitch two linen squares with a $\frac{1}{2}''$ seam leaving a 2″ opening for turning.
2. Trim and turn to the right side. Press. With wrong sides together, topstitch $\frac{3}{8}''$ from the seam leaving a 2″ opening in the same place as the previous stitching.

3. Fill with scented buckwheat. Slipstitch the remaining outside edge closed. Topstitch $\frac{3}{8}''$ from the edge closing the opening.
4. Repeat the process to complete the second and third pillows.
5. Stack the pillows on top of one another. Place the center of the ribbon across the top of the pillows and wrap around to the bottom of the stack. Wrap the ribbon ends around each other and around opposite sides of pillows to top.
6. Tie ribbon in a knot around a cinnamon stick on top of the pillow stack. Trim the ends of the ribbon at an angle. Insert velvet leaves in the knot and twist the wire stems to secure.

SURPRISE!

Materials:

- ¼ yard of cotton velvet
- 12″ of ⅝″ wide wire-edged ribbon
- Pattern "M"
- Pattern "N"
- Chalk marker
- Needle board or Velvet press cloth

1. Cut one piece of pattern "M" and two pieces of "N" out of cotton velvet.
2. Stitch $1/2$" inside all edges of "M".
3. Clip to stitching as marked on "M".
4. Place "M" on the needle board with the pile side down and press back the hems on "M".

5. Stitch $1/2$" inside all the edges of two "N" pieces.
6. Trim the corners of "N" diagonally.
7. Fold out the hems of "M". With right sides together, pin one "N" to the first section of one long edge of "M". Stitch together with a $1/2$" seam starting at the hem foldline of "M" and sinking the needle into the fabric at the first clip mark. Use the previous stitching as a guide.

8. With the needle in the fabric at the clip mark, pivot "N" and match up the second side with the long edge of "M". Continue stitching and pivoting until all four sides of "N" are stitched.
9. Repeat the process with the remaining "N" side stitching it to the other long side of "M".
10. Turn the cube right side out. Fill with scented buckwheat. Slipstitch the opening closed.
11. Make a bow from the wire-edged ribbon. Handstitch the bow to the center of one side of the cube.

COUCHED THREAD POTPOURRI PURSE

Materials:

- ¼ yard of metallic organza
- 1¼ yard each of six different decorative threads
- Metallic thread
- 10" of ⅝" wide ribbon
- Pattern "H"
- Pinking shears
- Braiding or cording foot
- Potpourri

1. Cut out one pattern "H" from the metallic organza.
2. Pink the edge of the marked hem on "H".
3. Cut the decorative threads into 14" lengths. Divide the threads into three groups of one of each type of thread.
4. Center one group of thread lengthwise on the right side of "H". Using a braiding foot and metallic thread, couch the decorative threads to the organza with a zig-zag stitch. Start stitching at the hem foldline and end stitching ½" inside the flap foldline. Satin stitch over the threads at the end to hold in place. Clip the ends of the threads 2" below satin stitches.

5. Repeat the process with the remaining decorative threads ½" from either side of the center couched threads.
6. With wrong sides together, fold along the hem foldline and topstitch in place ¼" away from the fold.

7. With right sides together, fold "H" along the top foldline.
8. With wrong sides together, fold "H" along the flap foldline.

9. With right sides together, fold "H" along the bag foldline.
10. Stitch the raw edges together with a ¼" seam.
11. Turn the bag to the right side. Fill with a small amount of potpourri.
12. Make a bow in the ⅝" wide ribbon. Stitch the bow to the center of the flap through all layers of the bag.

MASCULINE SACHET

Materials:

- ¼ yard of cotton flannel or shirting
- 1 - ¾" button
- Pattern "J"
- 1 - 16" x 6" rectangle of muslin
- ¼" or Quilting foot
- Balsam needles

1. Cut one piece of pattern "J" out of flannel. Serge finish the hem of "J" where shown. With the wrong sides of the fabric together, fold the serged edge back ½". Topstitch ⅜" away from the edge.
2. With right sides together, fold on foldline #1. Press. Sew a ¼" seam from the folded edge to the hemmed edge along the sides.

3. Serge finish the raw edges as shown.

4. Turn the pocket right side out. With right sides together, fold the flap in half. Stitch the top edge together with a 1/4" seam. Press the seam open.

5. Turn the flap to the right side and press the point flat. With wrong sides together, fold in 1/4" side seam allowances between the flap and the pocket. Press in place.

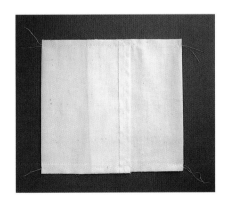

6. On the right side, topstitch 1/8" from the edge securing the side seam allowances and flap in place. Make a buttonhole in the point of the flap as marked.

7. Sew the button in place on the pocket as marked.

The Muslin Bag

8. Fold the short ends of the rectangle under 1/2" and zig-zag the fold in place 1/4" away from the edge.

9. With right sides together, fold the ends towards each other and overlap 2" in the center forming a 6 1/2" x 6" rectangle. Stitch the raw edges together with a 1/4" seam.

10. Trim and turn to the right side. Fill with balsam needles. Place the muslin bag in the sachet pocket and button the flap in place.

DRAWSTRING BAG

Materials:

- 1 - 16" circle of cut velvet
- 1 - 16" circle of matching silk
- 2' of ¹⁄₈" cord
- 4 beads with large holes
- Velvet press cloth
- Small safety pin
- Heat-Away™ stabilizer
- Walking foot
- Eyelet foot or attachment
- Potpourri

1. Attach eyelet foot and on right side of cut velvet circle sew one $3/8''$ eyelet centered $2^3/8''$ inside raw edge. Before sewing, place a small amount of Heat-Away™ stabilizer under the fabric.
2. Directly opposite the first eyelet, sew another eyelet centered $2^3/8''$ inside the raw edge. Before sewing, place a small amount of Heat-Away™ stabilizer under the fabric. Remove the stabilizer and cut open the eyelets.

3. With right sides together, stitch the fabric circles together with a $1/4''$ seam using a walking foot and leaving an 2″ opening for turning.
4. Turn to the right side and press using a velvet press cloth so as to not crush pile. Slipstitch the opening closed.

5. Stitch a circle through both layers of fabric approximately $2^3/8''$ inside the outside edge. The stitching should line up with the top of the eyelets.
6. Stitch a second circle through both layers of fabric approximately $2^3/4''$ inside the outside edge. The stitching should line up with the bottom of the eyelets.
7. Cut the cording into two 1 yard pieces. Attach a small safety pin to the end of one piece of cording. Thread the cord through the eyelet and into the casing and around the circle to feed out the same eyelet. Attach a small safety pin to the end of the remaining piece of cord. Thread the cord through the opposite eyelet, into the casing, around the circle and out the same eyelet.
8. Draw the bag up slightly distributing the gathers evenly. Fill with potpourri. Draw the bag opening closed. Wrap the drawstrings around the bag in opposite directions and tie in a bow.
9. Slip the beads on the ends of the cording and knot the cording below the bead. Fray the ends of the cording.

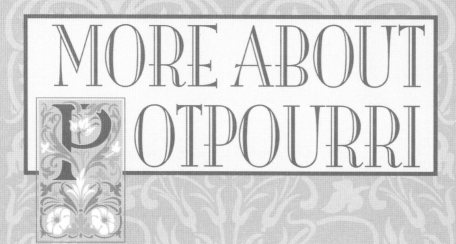

MORE ABOUT POTPOURRI

The quality of any potpourri is only as good as the components used to create it. The following is a list of ingredients that will yield the most successful results when creating a potpourri.

Flowers

anemone	lavender
bell flower	lily
calendula	malva
cornflower	peony
daffodil	pinks
delphinium	rose
geranium	statice
globe amaranth	strawflower
hibiscus	sunflower
iris	tilia
jonquil	violet
larkspur	

Leaves

bay leaf
balsam fir needles
box
eucalyptus
lemon grass
patchouli
rose leaves
uva ursi

Herbs

allspice
costmary
feverfew
lavender
lemon balm
lemon verbena
mint
rosemary
sage
salvia
thyme

Spices

chamomile
cloves
cinnamon
coriander
ginger root
orange peel
lemon peel
star anise

Fixatives

calamus root
cellulose fiber
gum benzoin
oak moss
orris root

ADDITIONAL POTPOURRI RECIPES

Sweet Dreams

3 cups - roses
2 cups - lavender
2 cups - chamomile
1 cup - marjoram
2 cups - hops
1/2 cup - lemon grass
1/2 cup - oak moss
1 ounce - lavender oil

Gypsy Rose

2 cups - roses
1 cup - cinnamon
1 cup - cloves
2 cups - sage
1 cup - rosemary
1 cup - lemon peel
1 cup - oak moss
1/2 ounce - rose oil
1/2 ounce - cedarwood oil

Citrus Potpourri

3 cups - orange peel
2 cups - lemon verbena
1 cup - chamomile
1/2 cup - coriander
1/2 cup - rosemary
2 cups - lemon grass
1 cup - orris root
1 ounce - lemon or lemon verbena oil

For additional sachet fabric and potpourri resource information in the United States, please send a SASE to Sewing Information Resources, Box 330, Wasco, IL 60183.

PATTERNS

ENVELOPE WRAP

1 square = 1/2"
Enlarge pattern 200%

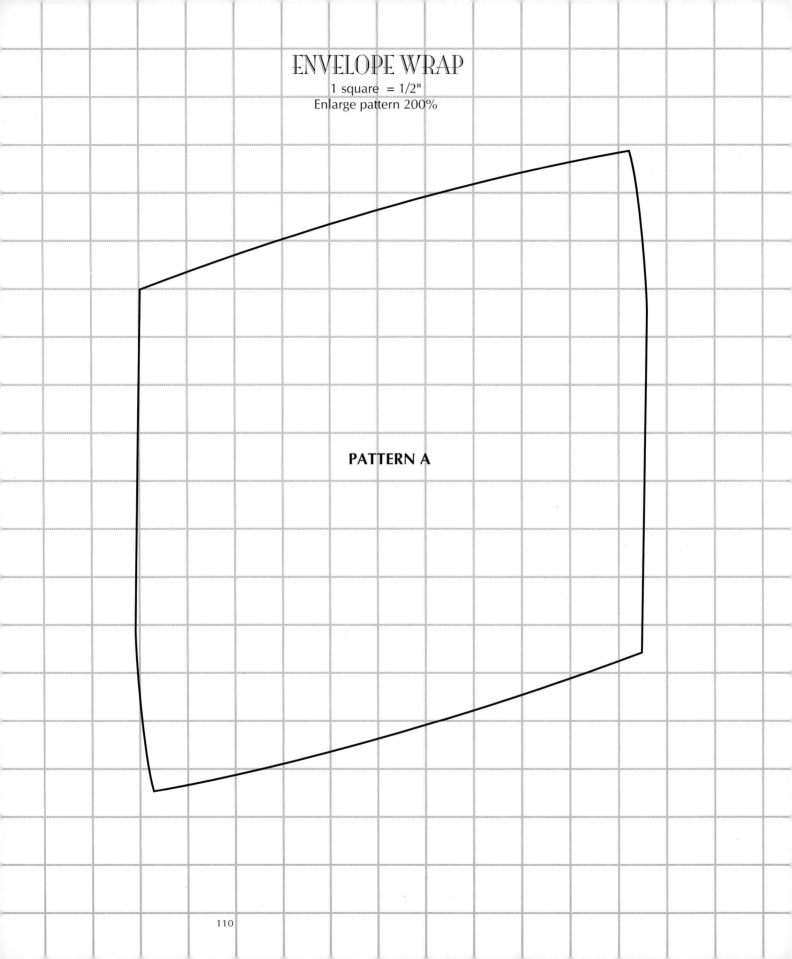

PATTERN A

SCENTED SHOE
STUFFERS

1 square = 1"
Actual Size

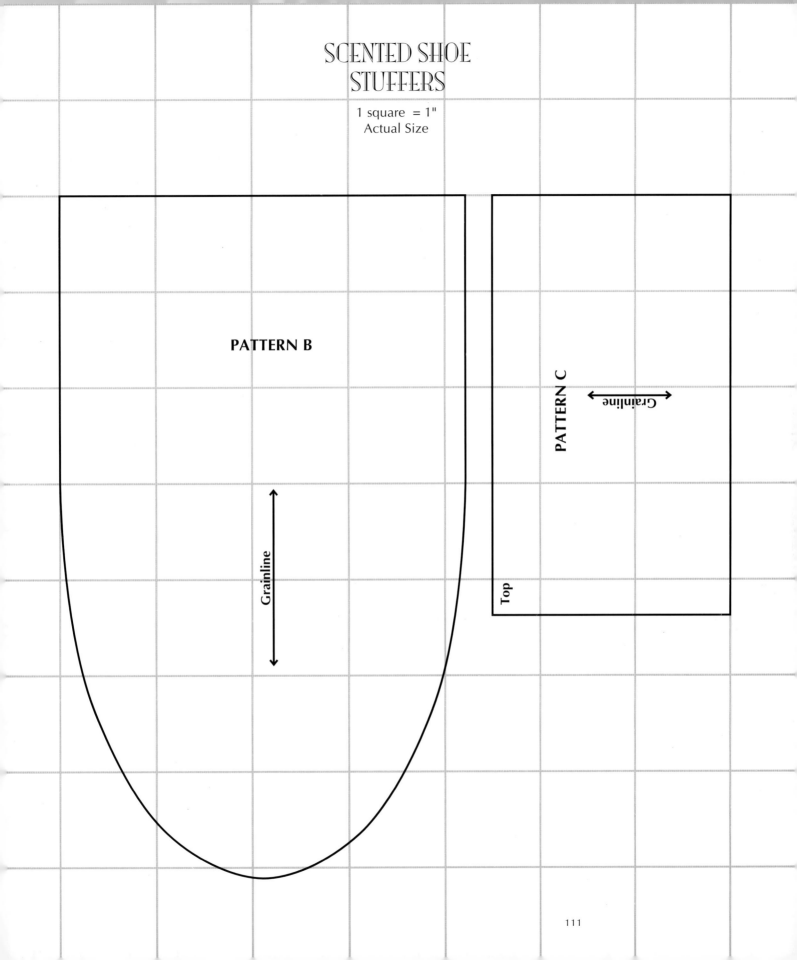

PATTERN B

Grainline

PATTERN C

Grainline

Top

EYELET TEMPLATE

1 square = 1"
Actual Size

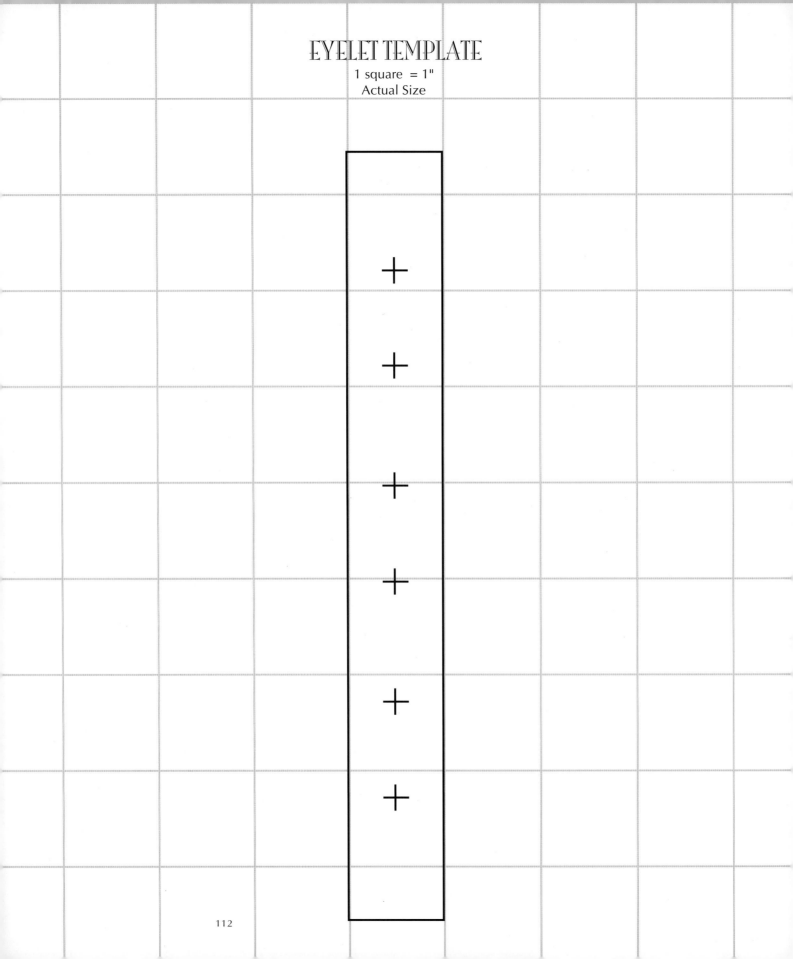

WOVEN HEART

1 square = 1"
Actual Size

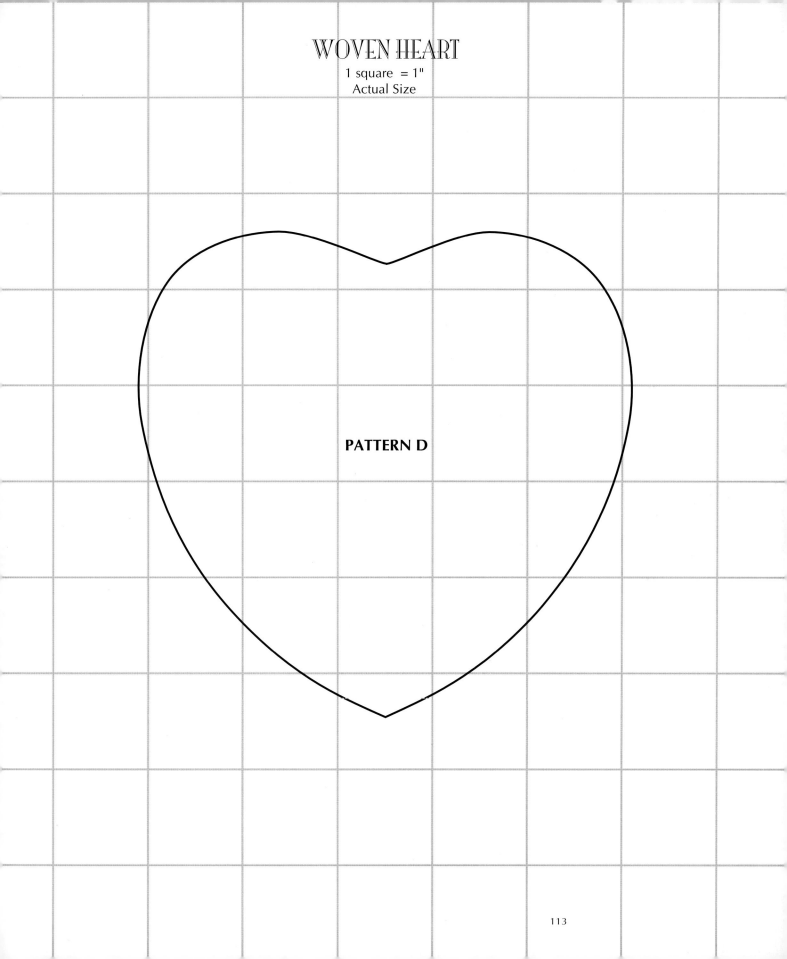

PATTERN D

HOLIDAY ORNAMENT

1 square = 1"
Actual Size

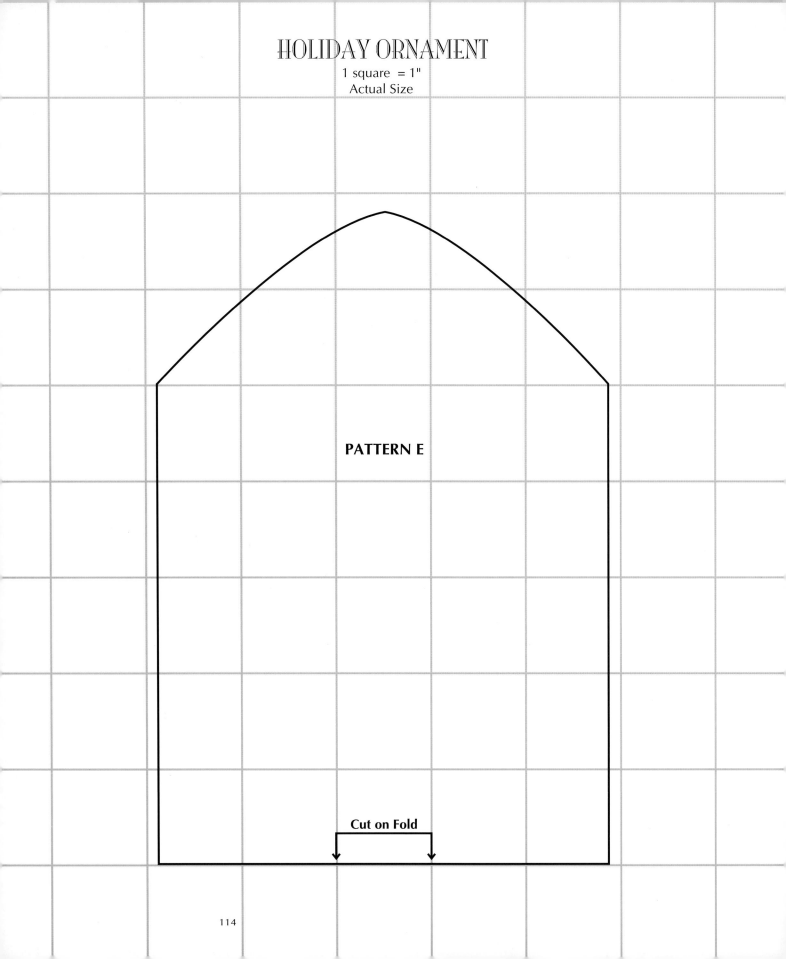

PATTERN E

Cut on Fold

114

HOLIDAY ORNAMENT

1 square = 1"
Actual Size

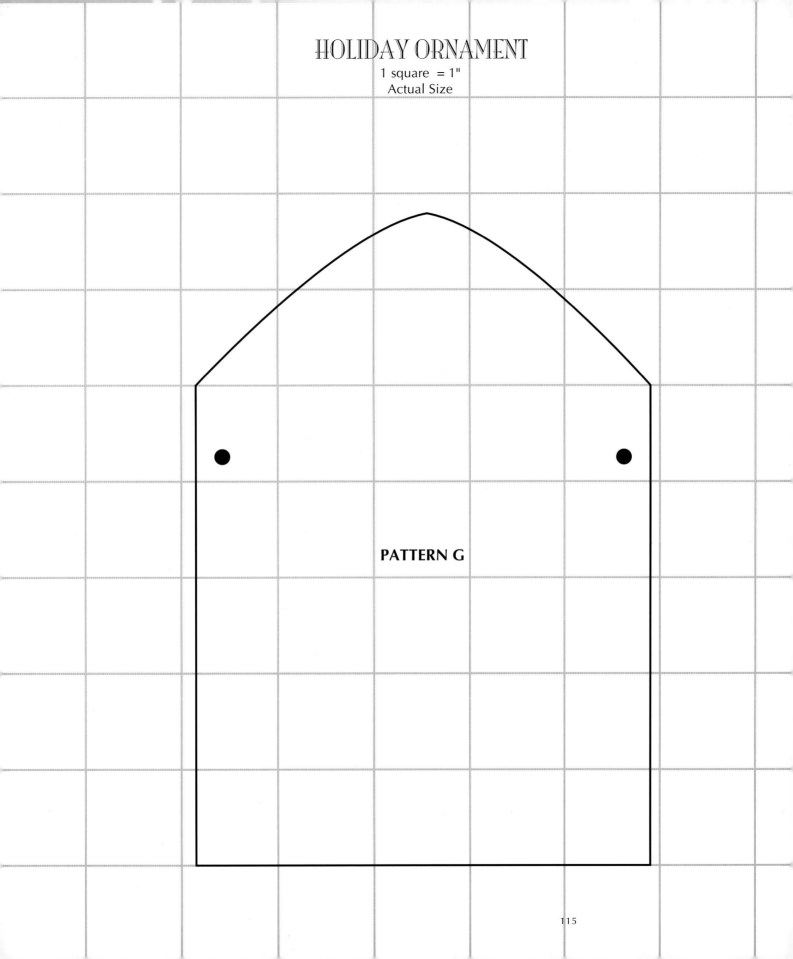

PATTERN G

COUCHED THREAD POTPOURRI PURSE

1 square = 1/2"

Enlarge pattern 200%

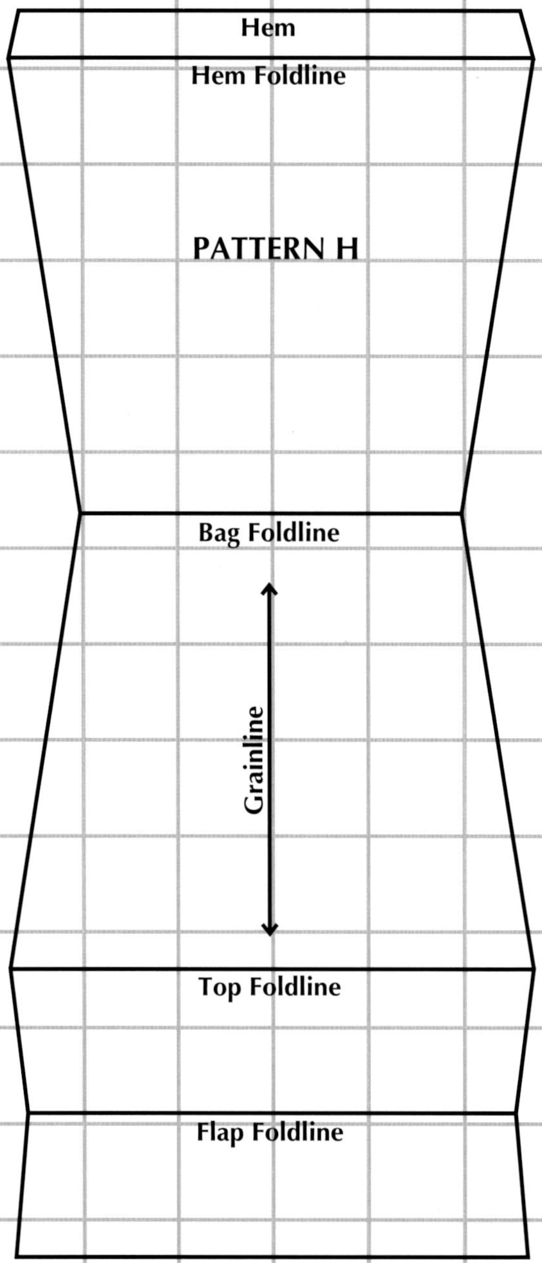

Hem

Hem Foldline

PATTERN H

Bag Foldline

Grainline

Top Foldline

Flap Foldline

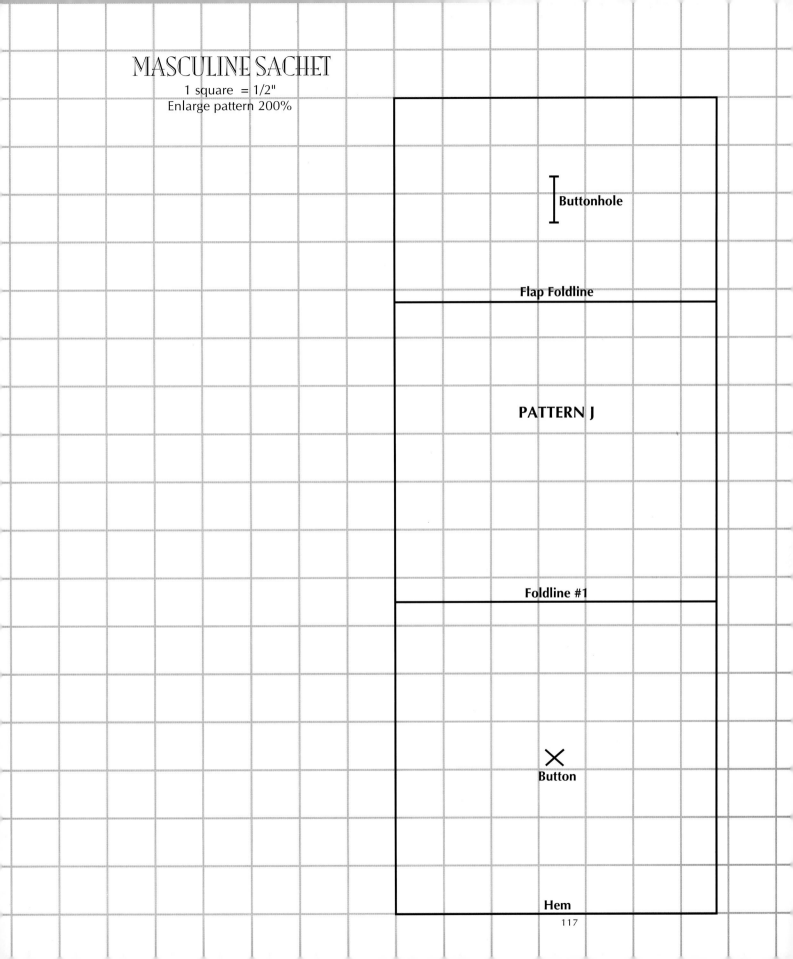

MASCULINE SACHET

1 square = 1/2"

Enlarge pattern 200%

Buttonhole

Flap Foldline

PATTERN J

Foldline #1

Button

Hem

SURPRISE!

1 square = 1/2"
Enlarge pattern 200%

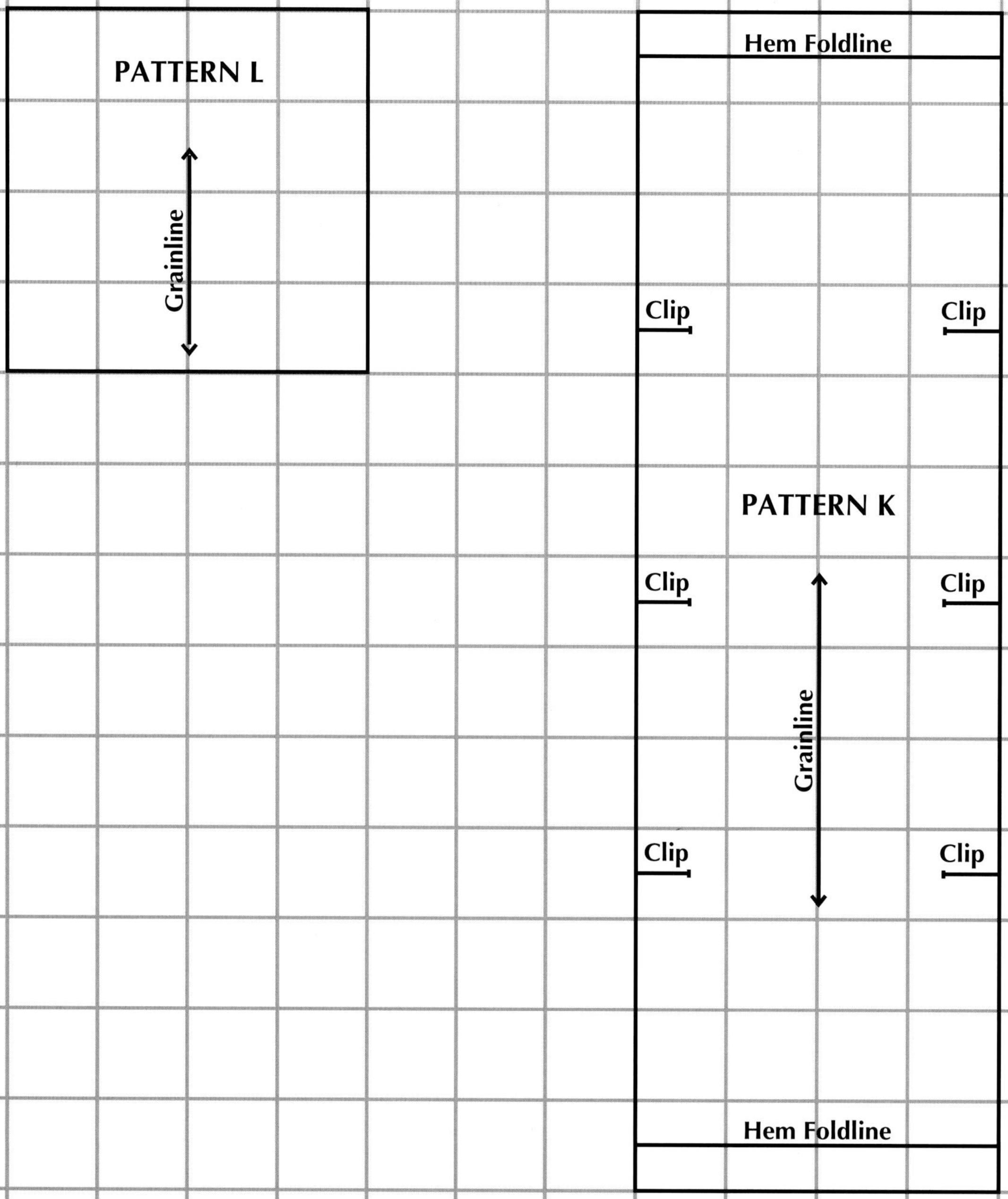

PATTERN L

Grainline

Hem Foldline

Clip

Clip

PATTERN K

Clip

Clip

Grainline

Clip

Clip

Hem Foldline

118

METRIC EQUIVALENTS

INCHES TO MILLIMETERS AND CENTIMETERS
MM—millimeters   CM—centimeters

Inches	MM	CM	Inches	CM	Inches	CM
1/8	3	0.3	9	22.9	30	76.2
1/4	6	0.6	10	25.4	31	78.7
3/8	10	1.0	11	27.9	32	81.3
1/2	13	1.3	12	30.5	33	83.8
5/8	16	1.6	13	33.0	34	86.4
3/4	19	1.9	14	35.6	35	88.9
7/8	22	2.2	15	38.1	36	91.4
1	25	2.5	16	40.6	37	94.0
1 1/4	32	3.2	17	43.2	38	96.5
1 1/2	38	3.8	18	45.7	39	99.1
1 3/4	44	4.4	19	48.3	40	101.6
2	51	5.1	20	50.8	41	104.1
2 1/2	64	6.4	21	53.3	42	106.7
3	76	7.6	22	55.9	43	109.2
3 1/2	89	8.9	23	58.4	44	111.8
4	102	10.2	24	61.0	45	114.3
4 1/2	114	11.4	25	63.5	46	116.8
5	127	12.7	26	66.0	47	119.4
6	152	15.2	27	68.6	48	121.9
7	178	17.8	28	71.1	49	124.5
8	203	20.3	29	73.7	50	127.0

METRIC CONVERSION CHART

Yards	Inches	Meters
$\frac{1}{8}$	4.5	0.11
$\frac{1}{4}$	9	0.23
$\frac{3}{8}$	13.5	0.34
$\frac{1}{2}$	18	0.46
$\frac{5}{8}$	22.5	0.57
$\frac{3}{4}$	27	0.69
$\frac{7}{8}$	31.5	0.80
1	36	0.91
$1\frac{1}{8}$	40.5	1.03
$1\frac{1}{4}$	45	1.14
$1\frac{3}{8}$	49.5	1.26
$1\frac{1}{2}$	54	1.37
$1\frac{5}{8}$	58.5	1.49
$1\frac{3}{4}$	63	1.60
$1\frac{7}{8}$	67.5	1.71
2	72	1.83

ABOUT THE AUTHOR

Stephanie Valley's passion for creating and designing led her to a degree in textile design from the University of Kansas. Throughout her career, she has produced one-of-a-kind silk-screened and hand-stamped fabric yardage and a variety of artistic pieces of clothing and accessories. She was the set stylist and prop director for the popular PBS television series, *Sewing Today.* Currently, Stephanie is the production director for The Sewing Workshop Pattern Collection, a boutique line of clothing patterns sold throughout the United States produced by The Sewing Workshop, San Francisco Ca.